Contents

dent

nfidence, you ... know when ... vise, you will never be moved to consult a reference manual; you'll assume that what you have written is correct as it stands.) Second, once you think you have encountered a potential problem, you need to know where to look for help. Third, once you have found the appropriate rule, you need to know how to apply it correctly to the specific problem you have found.

The *Comprehensive Worksheets for The Gregg Reference Manual,* Tenth Edition, has been specifically designed to help you build these three skills. First of all, these worksheets will familiarize you with the wide range of potential problems you are likely to encounter in punctuation, capitalization, number style, abbreviations, plural and possessive forms, spelling, compounds, word division, grammar, usage, and the format of letters, memos, reports, and other business documents. Second, these worksheets will direct you to the key rules in each section of *The Gregg Reference Manual* so that later on, when you encounter similar problems in your own work, you'll know where to look. Third, they will sharpen your ability to apply the rules correctly under many different circumstances.

There are 33 worksheets in all. Worksheet 1, the Diagnostic Survey, is a four-page unit that covers all the key points in *The Gregg Reference Manual.* It is intended to show you how much you already know, how good you are in looking things up on your own, and what sections of the manual you need to give special attention to. In addition to the items that focus on specific points, there are some sentences for you to rewrite and a full-page letter (covering a wide range of problems) for you to edit and retype.

Worksheets 2–28 focus on specific sets of rules within each section. They offer two special helps: (1) each exercise within a worksheet will tell you which set of rules you ought to review in advance; and (2) next to each answer blank you will find the specific rule number or numbers that apply to that answer. Within this sequence of worksheets you will find four special surveys that will help you integrate what you have learned from the ear-

lier materials. Thus, after you have completed Worksheets 2–6 (which focus on the proper use of punctuation), you will encounter Editing Survey A in Worksheet 7. Now, without the help of rule numbers in the margin, you will be asked to edit two extended passages of material. Whereas Worksheets 2–6 each acquainted you with small segments of punctuation rules in Sections 1–2 of *The Gregg Reference Manual,* you will now be expected to draw on all these rules as you edit the materials in Worksheet 7. In the same way, Editing Survey B in Worksheet 13 will ask you to apply all the rules in Sections 3–5 (on capitalization, numbers, and abbreviations), which you were gradually introduced to in Worksheets 8–12. Editing Survey C in Worksheet 20 deals with the problems covered in Sections 6–9 and Worksheets 14–19. Finally, Editing Survey D in Worksheet 25 deals with the grammar and usage guidelines presented in Sections 10–11 and applied in Worksheets 21–24.

When you get to Worksheets 29–32, you will encounter five letters, the continuation page of a letter, an envelope, a memo, and a page from a report—all of which incorporate a number of common problems drawn from all sections of the manual. In these worksheets no specific rule numbers will be given as aids. As a result of your training up to this point, you should now be able to identify the potential problems that exist, find the relevant rules on your own, and apply them correctly to each situation.

Worksheet 33, the Final Survey, exactly parallels the four-page Diagnostic Survey. It will give you the opportunity to demonstrate to your instructor—and more important, to yourself—the considerable gain in skill you have achieved by working your way through these worksheets.

How to Show Corrections. In many of the worksheets you will be asked to identify errors and make corrections within the line (rather than in an answer column). The chart of proofreaders' marks that appears on pages 358–359 of *The Gregg Reference Manual* (and also on the inside back cover) will show you how to indicate various kinds of corrections. Refer to the chart as necessary.

 **McGraw-Hill
Irwin**

**Comprehensive Worksheets to Accompany
THE GREGG REFERENCE MANUAL: A MANUAL OF STYLE, GRAMMAR, USAGE,
AND FORMATTING, Tenth Edition**
William A. Sabin

Published by McGraw-Hill/Irwin, a business unit of The McGraw-Hill Companies, Inc., 1221 Avenue of the Americas, New York, NY 10020. Copyright © 2005, 2001, 1996, 1992, 1985, 1977, 1970, 1961, 1956, 1951 by The McGraw-Hill Companies, Inc. All rights reserved. No part of this publication may be reproduced or distributed in any form or by any means, or stored in a database or retrieval system, without the prior written consent of The McGraw-Hill Companies, Inc., including, but not limited to, in any network or other electronic storage or transmission, or broadcast for distance learning.

6 7 8 9 0 WDQ/WDQ 0

ISBN 978-0-07-293655-1
MHID 0-07-293655-X

www.mhhe.com

The **McGraw·Hill** Companies

1

Diagnostic Survey

Directions: Correct the punctuation and capitalization in each sentence below. If the punctuation is incorrect, draw a line through it: *an old winter coat.* If new punctuation is to be inserted, circle it: *I too hope so.* To change a small letter to a capital letter, draw three lines under it: *Christmas.* To change a capital letter to a small letter, draw a line through it: *Enough.* If a sentence is correct as given, write *C* in the answer column. **References:** Sections 1–3.

1. Dawn Sam and I now use lightweight compact camcorders in our training sessions   1. _____
2. Could I please ask you to evaluate my manuscript by this Friday July 6   2. _____
3. I've just read your memo of March 2 which describes your committee's progress in updating the corporate guidelines on sexual harassment many thanks   3. _____
4. The General Manager of the Accounting department asked how much your new iMac cost   4. _____
5. Did we really win the bid for converting the old mill into condos fantastic   5. _____
6. It's funny isn't it how people with a push-button phone still listen for a dial tone   6. _____
7. Did the TV reporter who called friday night, leave her name and phone number   7. _____
8. In my opinion the Company's sales will triple by the year 2008   8. _____
9. While you're traveling next month could I please make use of your office   9. _____
10. I'm opening a fast-food outlet in Boise Idaho and if feasible one in Baker Oregon   10. _____
11. It is critical therefore that their President Rob Kidd cut out lavish corporate perks   11. _____
12. Sort the sales data as follows. By product type customer class and ZIP Code   12. _____
13. Sarah Hess M.B.A. has joined the Company, but will not relocate here until Fall   13. _____
14. Does the State have jurisdiction or must the case be tried in a Federal court   14. _____
15. When we went out West last Summer we stayed in an old, mining town   15. _____
16. Joe's holdings in the company must be worth at least $1250000 wouldn't you say   16. _____
17. We have therefore decided not to sell even though we got some good bids   17. _____
18. The partners tried to save the business but it folded on june 15 1999   18. _____
19. Is it true Ron that Harvey Snow the Chairman of CMP will run for public office   19. _____
20. In 2003 we almost hired Wim VanVliet Jr. of Tubbins Inc. for the job of CFO   20. _____
21. To operate the equipment turn the key to the right to stop it press the red panel   21. _____
22. After he accepted the settlement Gary said why didn't I ask for more   22. _____
23. (See chapter 3 the man with the gun in the book a time to be saved   23. _____
24. The new officers are: Sue Foy President Rob Henry Secretary and Jon Poe Treasurer   24. _____
25. Your figures look okay to me however please get the finance department's approval   25. _____
26. Is the Institute Of Management Consultants near Grand Central station   26. _____
27. She has written articles on american history, and politics in the twentieth century for example her thesis was on the great depression and the thirties   27. _____
28. After I lost my job I went back to Southern Ohio but I miss Washington D.C.   28. _____
29. Tony Nye along with his family flew to Rome to celebrate new year's eve   29. _____
30. An "ad hoc" committee was formed in June 2003 or was it 2004   30. _____

Directions: The following items deal with problems in number style, abbreviations, plural and possessive forms, spelling, compound words, and word division. (*Note:* The symbol / is used in items 96–100 to show word division at the end of a line.) If an item is correct as given, write *C* in the answer column. If an item is incorrect, circle the error and show the correct form in the answer column. **References:** Sections 4–9.

#	Item	Answer	#	Item	Answer
31.	six tapes and 15 CDs	_____	66.	prefered to relocate	_____
32.	no later than March 21st	_____	67.	creditted my account	_____
33.	priced under $100.00	_____	68.	used sound judgement	_____
34.	more than $.15 apiece	_____	69.	felt quite releived	_____
35.	. . . said yes. 12 said no.	_____	70.	required assistence	_____
36.	early in the 21st century	_____	71.	is now superceded	_____
37.	nearly 2/3 occupied	_____	72.	retype your resumé	_____
38.	sold in eight-ounce cans	_____	73.	the details don't jibe	_____
39.	until I turned five	_____	74.	more then we need	_____
40.	a 15-year mortgage	_____	75.	it's to far to go	_____
41.	more than 20 years ago	_____	76.	look for a concensus	_____
42.	starts at seven P.M.	_____	77.	after next Febuary	_____
43.	heard from B.J. Malone	_____	78.	serve as liason	_____
44.	referred by Doctor Milano	_____	79.	discussed publically	_____
45.	an F.B.I. investigation	_____	80.	just read the summery	_____
46.	US Department of Labor	_____	81.	too much paperwork	_____
47.	works in Washington, D.C.	_____	82.	I'll follow-up on it	_____
48.	8 yds. @ $2.75	_____	83.	review these print-outs	_____
49.	a tolerance of 2 mm.	_____	84.	time for decision making	_____
50.	an IRS audit	_____	85.	likes it single spaced	_____
51.	not many vacancys	_____	86.	high risk investments	_____
52.	talk to my attornies	_____	87.	a nine-month's schedule	_____
53.	built additional shelfs	_____	88.	a real estate syndicate	_____
54.	both my brothers-in-law	_____	89.	a tax exempt purchase	_____
55.	use only one criteria	_____	90.	becomes habit forming	_____
56.	called the Peabodies	_____	91.	too high priced for me	_____
57.	throughout the 1990's	_____	92.	a clearly written draft	_____
58.	can't read my boss' notes	_____	93.	is this up-to-date	_____
59.	bought Ed Jone's house	_____	94.	need to re-emphasize	_____
60.	both agencies' assets	_____	95.	is rather self serving	_____
61.	womens' compensation	_____	96.	they plan-/ ned poorly	_____
62.	it's Daisy's, not our's	_____	97.	sim-/ ilar conditions	_____
63.	Mark and Tom's allergies	_____	98.	contin-/ uous motion	_____
64.	bought six dollars worth	_____	99.	recall-/ ing the past	_____
65.	talk about us buying a car	_____	100.	compell-/ ing reasons	_____

2

Directions: Underline all errors and write the correct forms in the answer column. If a sentence is correct as given, write *C* in the answer column. **References:** Sections 10–11.

101.	Every videocassette and compact disc are now on sale.	101. _____
102.	Not one of the photocopiers are working properly.	102. _____
103.	Does any of the orders call for out-of-stock items?	103. _____
104.	Some criteria on eligibility for outplacement services has to be established.	104. _____
105.	The number of responses to our mail campaign were unusually high.	105. _____
106.	Diane is one of those managers who always resolves problems quickly.	106. _____
107.	None of the bidders have handled this big a project before.	107. _____
108.	I wish I was free to work with you on the Henderson case.	108. _____
109.	Can the company maintain their dominant position in the marketplace?	109. _____
110.	Apparently, everyone on staff has been notified except you and I.	110. _____
111.	You obviously know a good deal more about this new technology than me.	111. _____
112.	Valerie and myself are the only ones who still report to Mrs. Lee.	112. _____
113.	Whom do you think is going to get the Hong Kong assignment?	113. _____
114.	We had a real nice going-away party for Celia Frazier.	114. _____
115.	I felt very badly about George's decision to retire.	115. _____
116.	I don't see nothing wrong with the plan you have devised.	116. _____
117.	What affect will the increased sales tax have on your firm?	117. _____
118.	We've had a great amount of calls on the basis of one ad.	118. _____
119.	I'm afraid we won't have more stock on Model 364-A for awhile.	119. _____
120.	You need to work for greater precision and less mistakes.	120. _____

Directions: Rewrite the following sentences to correct all errors. **References:** Primarily Sections 10–11.

121. Every businessman should review his objectives continuously._____

_____

122. They not only plan to audit this years' records but also last year. _____

_____

123. Neither the salesclerks nor the sales manager has received his bonus check. _____

_____

124. When taking a trip, money can be saved. If reservations are made in advance. _____

_____

125. The contract's terms have been carefully reviewed by everyone of us._____

_____

Directions: On the reverse side of this sheet you will find a letter to **Ms. Gina A. Hodgkins** (typed in modified-block style—standard format with standard punctuation). Correct all errors in style, grammar, and format; also look for errors in typing and content. Circle all changes you make within the lines or out in the margins; if you prefer, show all changes on a separate sheet, identified by line number. If time permits, retype the corrected letter on a plain sheet of paper, using 1.25-inch side margins and positioning the date on the first line below a 2-inch top margin. **References:** Section 13 plus Sections 1–12. See also pages 358–359 or the inside back cover of *The Gregg Reference Manual* for a chart showing how to indicate corrections on typed material.

Seco Valley Inn

Post Office Box 151 - Sonoma, California 95476
Telephone: (707) 555-9850 - Fax: (707) 555-9867 E-Mail: svi@aol.com

Aug. 7 2007

Gina A. Hodgkins
Director of administrative services,
Robb, Steele & Baggett
Suite 1,950
612 W. 6th St.
Los Angeles, CA, 90017

Dear Ms. Hodgekin,

Thank you very much for you letter of August 2nd in which you expressed an interest in bringing the partners in your law firm to Seco Valley
Inn for their annual retreat later this Fall. We would be delighted to
serve you and your associates in anyway that we can. Let me try to answer the questions you asked in your letter.

1 It will take you about an hour or 2 to drive from the Airport South
of San Fransisco to the inn, depending on the time of day you come across
the Golden Gate bridge.

2 A 36 hole golf course surrounds the inn. Also readily accessible are
eight all weather tennis courts, a fully-equipped exercise room and in
and outdoor swimming pools.

3 Room service is available from 6:00 am-11:00 pm. The Coffee Garden
provides a causal menu throughout the day and the Elbow Room offers an
elegant award wining menu for lunch and dinner.

   I am enclosing a brochure, that describes all our facilitys in
greater detail. Also enclosed is a schedule of our room rates and a
reservation form on which you can indicate the accomodations you want.
All of us here at Seco Valley Inn look foreward to serving you.

                                        Sincerly your's

                                        Lyle A. Montoya
                                        General Manager

Enclosure 1
gad

4

2 The Period, the Question Mark, and the Exclamation Point

Directions: Supply the appropriate mark of punctuation at the end of each sentence and circle it. If no additional punctuation is required, write *C* in the answer column. **References:** ¶¶101–121.

1. I want to thank you for the fine job you did on the Miller-Jacobs study

    1. _____ 101a

2. May I please get your thoughts on how the seminar should be structured

    2. _____ 103a

3. May I invite outside speakers to participate in the seminar

    3. _____ 103b

4. I doubt whether you can find a flight that leaves before 6:30 a.m.

    4. _____ 101a

5. Does the CEO really expect the staff to buy that story? Incredible

    5. _____ 119a

6. Would you please have the bill sent to my home address

    6. _____ 103a

7. Would you please take care of my cats while I'm away for a month

    7. _____ 103b

8. Why don't you shift your advertising account to Bell, Buch, and Kendall Inc.

    8. _____ 110a

9. The only remaining question is, Do the benefits justify the risks

    9. _____ 115

10. The only remaining question is whether the benefits justify the risks

    10. _____ 115

11. Be sure to verify any figures that Harry Hanks comes up with

    11. _____ 101a

12. May I suggest that you talk to your lawyer before signing this contract

    12. _____ 103a

13. I would like to ask why the Bolling project is 50 percent over budget

    13. _____ 104

14. What do you make of this phrase—"at a date to be specified"

    14. _____ 110a

15. I can rely on your support at the board meeting, can't I

    15. _____ 114a

16. I question the wisdom of doing business with a company called Quality Ltd.

    16. _____ 101a

17. To obtain a copy, would you please send us a stamped, self-addressed envelope

    17. _____ 103a

18. Would you let me keep the battery of your BMW charged while you're gone

    18. _____ 103b

19. The sales manager has asked when Model GRX-10 will be back in stock

    19. _____ 104

20. When do you expect to receive your M.B.A.? Next year

    20. _____ 111

21. Now, to return to the main point of my argument

    21. _____ 101b

22. Would you please let us know whether we can do anything more to help you

    22. _____ 103a

23. Could you please arrange to have all the papers ready for me by Friday

    23. _____ 103b

24. You need to deal with the question of how much money you can afford to risk

    24. _____ 115

25. Why not consult your accountant and ask her for her opinion

    25. _____ 110b

26. Where the newspaper got its information will be revealed in tomorrow's issue

    26. _____ 104

27. Has anyone thought about the page design? the font? the type size

    27. _____ 117

28. The action we need to take is obvious; the question is how to break it to the members of the staff

    28. _____ 104

29. We still have the right, do we not, to terminate the agreement in thirty days

    29. _____ 114a

30. We just read about your graduating *summa cum laude.* Congratulations

    30. _____ 120

Name _____ Date _____ Class _____

Directions: Rewrite the following sentences to correct all errors in punctuation and to eliminate sentence fragments. Change the capitalization as necessary. **References:** ¶¶101–121. Also see ¶101c for a brief discussion of sentence fragments.

31. Be sure to proofread the originals carefully. Before you run off 250 copies. _____
    _____ 101a
    101c

32. Did you actually tell your boss that you didn't want the promotion, why?_____
    _____ 110a
    111

33. Is it true that you're planning to move back East, when, where?_____
    _____ 117

34. Why don't you call the box office? To see whether there are any seats left. _____
    _____ 110a
    101c

35. You can estimate, can't you?, how many units you expect to sell this year._____
    _____ 114a

Directions: Supply missing periods, question marks, and exclamation points. Change the capitalization as necessary. Circle all changes you make. **References:** ¶¶101–121.

36. The objectives of this special exercise program are:

    1 To teach you new techniques of relaxation

    2 To restore your energy and your sense of well-being   106
    107

37. *Illustration caption:* Figure 2-6 Federal Reserve Discount Rate Changes   108

38. I bought a quilt in your store about a week ago however, it doesn't go with the color scheme in my bedroom will you please refund my money when I return it   101a
    103b

39. You asked whether I would consider forming a partnership with you and your two brothers by all means   104
    101b
    119a

40. Jack reports that we did twice as much business this year at the jewelry show as we did last year unbelievable how do you account for it   101a
    119a
    110a

41. How we can get our candidate elected is the big question we can count on your backing, can't we   116
    114a

42. Why not rent a videocassette from our extensive collection of new releases better yet, buy one outright our prices are so low that they'll seem unbelievable   110b
    101a
    119

43. Will you please make sure that all the managers attend the special meeting set for this Friday I want to ask how we can cut costs without affecting quality   103a
    104

44. I want Martha Bradley to have the divisional sales reports as soon as possible will you please send her a copy of the printouts by messenger many thanks   101a
    103a
    101b

45. May we ask for your help would you be willing to contribute $20 to send a city child to camp this summer think about it, won't you   103b
    110a
    114a

46. I hear that Anne Bonney has seen an advance copy of my new book what did Mrs. B think of the coverage the organization my writing style   101a
    109a
    117

6

3

The Comma

Directions: Supply missing commas and strike out inappropriate commas in the following sentences. Circle all changes you make. If a sentence is correct as given, write *C* in the answer column. **References:** ¶¶122–125 (the basic comma rules).

1. The new warehouse has to be completed as I understand it by the end of the year. Your people can finish the job by then can't they?

   1. _____ 122a / 122b

2. It is obvious however that you cannot complete the work by December 31. We are therefore proceeding to cancel the contract.

   2. _____ 122c

3. *Newsweek* carried a review of your wife's new book *Managing Your Spouse* in the past month or so. The issue was dated September 19 2001 I believe.

   3. _____ 122d / 122e / 122b

4. Dean Morgan Hennessy Ed.D. will be speaking at an educational symposium in Knoxville Tennessee on stress, and teacher burnout in the classroom.

   4. _____ 122f / 125f

5. Luke Wharton II has been named to the newly established position of vice president and creative director of R. U. Kidd Inc.

   5. _____ 122f

6. Marla and I have already signed up for the Caribbean cruise but Sandy Peg and Bud are still mulling the trip over.

   6. _____ 123a / 123b

7. A lot of creativity and time and hard work went into developing all these handsome imaginative layouts.

   7. _____ 123b / 123c

8. Only $24000 is required on the signing of the contract; $216000 on the completion of the project.

   8. _____ 123d / 123e

9. When I graduated from business school in 2001 I hung out my shingle as a corporate turnaround expert. In order to deal with the extraordinary demand for my services I had to hire three associates in the very first year.

   9. _____ 124

10. You see I've worked with that pair on a number of projects. How they ever got their reputation for competence I'll never know.

    10. _____ 124a / 123e

11. In 2002 we established a new set of terms from credit card purchases. In my judgment those terms are now outdated and need to be rethought.

    11. _____ 124b / 122a

12. Our whole staff, I am sure will appreciate your kind words.

    12. _____ 125a

13. Margaret Pierce always turns in competent, well-written, research papers. Obviously she is ready for bigger things.

    13. _____ 125c / 124b

14. I'm sure I heard the commissioner say "These rate increases will be approved." However his assistant says that he did not.

    14. _____ 125b / 124b

15. We hope that you will find the meeting facilities satisfactory, and that you will tell us about any special needs. Our staff of course is always on call.

    15. _____ 125f / 122c

Directions: Supply missing commas and strike out inappropriate commas in the following sentences. Correct run-on sentences (see ¶128) by changing punctuation and capitalization as necessary. Circle all changes you make. If a sentence is correct as given, write *C* in the answer column. **References:** ¶¶126–137 plus the basic comma rules (¶¶122–125).

16.	Either the contract must be renegotiated or we must find another supplier.	**16.** _____	126a
17.	We must either renegotiate the contract or find another supplier.	**17.** _____	127b
18.	Give Jamie whatever data you've assembled and let her finish the analysis.	**18.** _____	127c
19.	You handle the names from A to M, I'll take care of N to Z.	**19.** _____	128
20.	I handle creative assignments and my partner runs the business.	**20.** _____	129
21.	If the meeting starts at 8 a.m. I will have to fly in the night before.	**21.** _____	130a
22.	However you want to organize the all-day meeting will be fine with me.	**22.** _____	130c
23.	My accountant warned me that, before I accepted the financial settlement, I had better consider the tax implications of the arrangement.	**23.** _____	130d
24.	This policy applies to employees who have less than six months of service.	**24.** _____	131a
25.	Jason Argonne whom I met on a flight to Warsaw turns out to be the uncle of the young woman who is engaged to marry your son.	**25.** _____	131b 131a
26.	Most customers when asked to take a blindfold test could not distinguish the taste of one cola from another.	**26.** _____	131c
27.	I sense that Ben Frost is trustworthy even though I have never dealt with him before.	**27.** _____	132
28.	This year's convention takes place in Portland Maine at the end of May but if you come a week early we can easily work in a trip to Nova Scotia.	**28.** _____	122f 133 132 130a
29.	Having observed how Joe handles the bids I think I can cover for him.	**29.** _____	135a
30.	Finding an affordable apartment in this city is not easy.	**30.** _____	135a
31.	To receive our highest discount you must order a minimum of 500 units.	**31.** _____	135b
32.	In all the years I worked for Mrs. Stebbins I never saw her smile.	**32.** _____	135c
33.	On weekdays we are open till 8 p.m., on Saturdays we close at 6 p.m.	**33.** _____	135c 128
34.	The president has announced that out of respect for the memory of Mr. Zucherman the office will be closed on Friday.	**34.** _____	136a
35.	What you should do in the meantime is review for the exam.	**35.** _____	137a
36.	What you should do in my opinion is review for the exam.	**36.** _____	122c 137b
37.	We would like you to speak for about thirty minutes, after a coffee break there will be time for questions and answers.	**37.** _____	128 135c 136a
38.	At the meeting in Dallas I ran into Ben Hurly who is now with Gasport and spent a few hours recalling old times.	**38.** _____	135c 131b
39.	While I was in graduate school I had to struggle to get through my courses whereas my roommate seemed to coast toward his doctorate.	**39.** _____	130a 132
40.	I'd be willing to meet next week but considering the amount of work you need to do in advance why don't we get together sometime in the following week?	**40.** _____	126a 127a 127d 136a

The Comma (Continued)

Directions: Supply missing commas and strike out inappropriate commas in the following sentences. Circle all changes you make. If a sentence is correct as given, write *C* in the answer column. **References:** ¶¶138–175 plus the basic comma rules (¶¶122–125) and the rules on clauses and phrases (¶¶126–137).

1. As a rule we can go from the drawing board to the marketplace in less than a year. There are times of course when it takes a little longer.

   1. _____ 139a / 141

2. Thus you can now afford an in-ground swimming pool too.

   2. _____ 139b / 143a

3. The advertising director along with the marketing managers will present next year's plans on Monday November 5 at 2 p.m.

   3. _____ 146a / 148

4. The word *parameter* is often misused by people who should know better.

   4. _____ 149

5. Thank you for your letter of December 12 in which you expressed a number of reservations about my new book *After the Millennium.*

   5. _____ 152 / 148 / 149

6. Doris Morley according to our personnel files served as promotion director from May 2002 until June 30 2004 the date she resigned.

   6. _____ 122a / 155a / 154a

7. Honorary degrees were awarded yesterday to Wilford B. Williams Esq. and Sarah Kennedy Millstein trustees of Collingwood University.

   7. _____ 157 / 148

8. If you want to reach me while I'm on vacation write to me at this address: Arrowhead Inn 106 Mason Road Durham North Carolina 27712.

   8. _____ 130a / 161 / 167

9. Two aspirin, and some strong black coffee always fix me up.

   9. _____ 168

10. To sum up these marketing strategies need to be rethought.

    10. _____ 139a / 175a

11. In short I think Marianne Yates has the appropriate skills and experience and in my opinion she ought to be promoted.

    11. _____ 139a / 126a / 142b / 124b

12. Well he is the shrewdest, although not the pleasantest person, I know.

    12. _____ 144a

13. Dr. Eileen Fahey head of the Halston Health Clinic will retire this year.

    13. _____ 148

14. A parenthetical or nonessential expression should be set off by appropriate punctuation that is by two commas within a sentence or by one comma at the beginning or end of a sentence.

    14. _____ 151 / 148

15. On April 21 2006 we initiated discussions with Llewellyn Perkins of the Micropro Company in Irvine California concerning the acquisition of his software business.

    15. _____ 154a / 153 / 160

16. Hastings-McConnell Inc. will hold a dinner-dance at the Glen Ridge New Jersey Country Club in honor of Weldon Wright Jr.'s retirement. *(Both the company and Mr. Wright use commas in their names.)*

    16. _____ 159 / 160 / 156

17. However you want to reorganize your group is entirely your decision.

    17. _____ 139a

18. Senators Allen Barlow and Cantor all agree that the state's methods for financing public education are unfair that the way funds are distributed is inequitable and that a special panel should investigate fairer approaches.

18. _____ 162a

19. The more Mr. Felker attacks the plan the more Mrs. Ketcham seems to endorse it. I think that we ought to get Mr. Glenn rather than Mr. Felker to point out the disadvantages of the plan to her. And the faster the better.

19. _____ 172d 147 172d

20. I'd like to recommend Fred that you recruit a new controller. The auditors I am sorry to say have discovered serious lapses in Don Springer's performance.

20. _____ 145 144

21. My wife Monica and I myself were part of the ecstatic crowd that gave the tenor Thomas Hampson a standing ovation for his performance as Figaro.

21. _____ 150 169

22. Our long-term, financial, situation now looks much much better than it did a few, short months ago.

22. _____ 171 175c 169

23. A great many ambitious career-minded employees have signed up for Mrs. Horowitz's popular English communications seminar.

23. _____ 170

24. The first three letters should be referred to Customer Service for handling; the other five to the Accounts Receivable Department.

24. _____ 172a

25. Jim now feels that whatever he does does not count for anything with the people he reports to.

25. _____ 175b

26. You, too, can qualify for this low-cost, easy-to-obtain, automobile, insurance if you are over 25, and have a clean, driving record for the past, three years.

26. _____ 143b 170 171 125f 167 169

27. I am pleased to be able to tell you Mr. Berger that the camcorder, which you ordered, is finally back in stock. You can pick one up at the store or if you prefer have it delivered to your home.

27. _____ 145 131a 122a

28. If however you and your partner Louis Meltzer prefer to lease the property rather than buy it outright I think I can persuade the owners to agree to that kind of arrangement.

28. _____ 142c 148 130a

29. On a trip to London Ontario I met an old friend of yours Roy Galt III who is the managing director of Cheswick and Forster Ltd. *(Styling preferences of Galt and the firm Cheswick and Forster are unknown.)*

29. _____ 160a 148 156 159

30. Please remember a team of five people has already invested many many hours not to mention thousands of dollars in studying the commercial applications of this new compound.

30. _____ 124a 175c 144

31. To scrub the project at this time when the first, useful data is being uncovered would come as a crushing disappointment.

31. _____ 148 169

32. We would, therefore, recommend that the present vacation policy be extended, until we can investigate what other companies in our industry are doing.

32. _____ 141 132

5 The Semicolon, the Colon, and the Comma

Directions: Supply missing punctuation and strike out or correct inappropriate punctuation in the following sentences. Change the capitalization as necessary. Circle all changes you make. If a sentence is correct as given, write *C* in the answer column. **References:** ¶¶176–199 (on the semicolon and the colon) plus ¶¶122–175 (on the comma).

1. My wife thinks we should move to Maine, I myself prefer to stay where we are.

   1. _____ 176a

2. We need to resolve our differences within the next ten days otherwise I'll take our business to another order fulfillment company.

   2. _____ 178

3. We have a number of objections to the draft of the agreement for example it fails to state by what date you will complete the construction.

   3. _____ 181a

4. As a rule, I don't take on malpractice cases, but given the facts as you present them, I would be pleased to represent you.

   4. _____ 139a 177c 136a

5. The entire labor dispute boils down to one issue namely who will set the standards of productivity?

   5. _____ 181b

6. Watch out for words that contain silent letters for example *autumn mortgage subpoena ophthalmologist.*

   6. _____ 182a

7. Three of our biggest accounts namely Fearoff-Lyon the Porterry Co. and Worth & Worth have submitted strong protests about our plans to close the distribution center in their state.

   7. _____ 183

8. I plan to call on clients in the following locations Shawnee Mission Kansas La Crosse Indiana and Fond du Lac Wisconsin.

   8. _____ 189 160a 184

9. The Vreeland property looks like a good buy the asking price seems in line with the assessed value and the buildings have all been maintained in excellent condition.

   9. _____ 187 197 167

10. The Vreeland property looks like a good buy however I'd like more data on the zoning laws and the tax rates before I make an offer.

    10. _____ 178 182b

11. We need only one final piece to the puzzle namely the source of the rumor.

    11. _____ 188

12. Those representatives in the Southern Region who exceeded their sales goals by more than 10 percent were: Amanda Collins Sue Ellen Mobley and Paul Cox.

    12. _____ 191c 162a 187

13. The consultants each identified the same problem we are understaffed.

    13. _____ 197

14. In short here is what the management consultant told me the business will need a cash infusion of $200,000 at once the business also needs an experienced manager to oversee the day-to-day operations.

    14. _____ 139a 187 199a 176

Name _____ Date _____ Class _____

Directions: Supply missing commas, semicolons, and colons as well as the appropriate punctuation at the end of each sentence. Change any incorrect punctuation already supplied. Change the capitalization as necessary. Circle all changes you make. **References:** ¶¶176–199 plus ¶¶101–175.

15. Thank you for your get-well card I am still confined to bed but I have been assured that the hip replacement was a complete success I expect to be up and about in another week, and to be calling on customers within a month

176b
126a
101a
125f
101a

16. The Gephardt estimate is not as high as it looks on the contrary the amount Gephardt is asking is about the same as the estimate from Kitchens Inc. in fact if you analyze the estimates closely Gephardt's is better because of the longer guarantee

178
139a
130a
101a

17. Natalie's memo explains why we ran out of stock yet it does not address the question of how we can avoid running out of stock again

179
104

18. As it happens I have a number of reservations about the Hepler Associates market survey for example why did they send questionnaires only to people who own their own homes

130a
181a
110

19. I'll be traveling first to Klamath Falls Oregon then I'll be going on to Bellingham Washington if the negotiations go faster than I've been assuming I may drive up to visit friends in Prince George British Columbia

160a
128
178
101a
130a

20. Mr. Workman from The Furniture Recyclers wants to know whether you are selling the desks and chairs individually or as a total package whether the stockroom shelves the lighting fixtures and the filing cabinets are also for sale and whether his drivers can come to collect any of these items before Wednesday September 28

186
162a
148
104

21. When selecting a format for a report consider the following factors
    1 For whom are you writing the report
    2 What outcome do you hope to achieve
    3 What is the existing mind-set of your reader

130b
189
106
107
110

22. Dear Mrs. Warnecke,

    Thank you for sending us your proposal for a book entitled *How to Start a Successful Business A Practical Guide for Entrepreneurs* would you be able to send us two sample chapters that we can evaluate moreover could you please tell us how long the complete manuscript is likely to run

194a
195a
101a
110
139a
103a

192
148
110

23. Why don't we discuss this matter at lunch at 1230 on Monday the 14th of April

24. I'll proceed to make reservations for us at Thai Won An: a charming restaurant at 19 Pacific Avenue do let me know if you prefer some other arrangement won't you

148
101a
114a

25. I'll be glad to reschedule our lunch if that proves necessary however I should note that since I'll be leaving the following day on a two-week business trip I won't be able to see you until after the first of May

132
101a
139a
130d
101a

6 Other Marks of Punctuation

Directions: Supply missing punctuation and strike out or correct inappropriate punctuation in the following sentences. Change the capitalization as necessary. Circle all changes you make. **References:** ¶¶201–226 (on the dash and parentheses) and ¶299. For guidance on how to show corrections in these sentences, see the chart on pages 358–359 or the inside back cover of *The Gregg Reference Manual.*

1. Here's a year-round vacation house that's ideal for you and your family; and at a price you can afford! 207

2. Chapter 8 discusses the techniques that can make regional marketing work for your company (see pages 86–89 220

3. Family that's what justifies the struggle to make this business succeed. 210

4. On all expense account items over $25, please be sure to provide a) a dated receipt and b) an explanation of the business purpose served by the expense. 222a

5. Three parts of olive oil, one part of vinegar, and one part of pure maple syrup that's all you need to make an outstanding salad dressing. 211b

6. Al Riesman (He's the marketing guru we frequently consult.) thinks that the approach we're taking in our new advertising campaigns is a total disaster. 224b 224c

7. Enclosed are the layouts for the catalog,—just the way you wanted them. 213

8. I thought we had agreed on a formula for compensation in the event the project is terminated before completion. (See your letter dated June 6). 226c

9. We will need the large meeting room we had last year—you will surely remember the one I mean—otherwise, we will have to break into two groups. 215c

10. In two weeks — October 4, to be exact — the President's panel is expected to release its recommendations on a national health insurance plan. 216a 299

11. Once a week (on Thursday nights we stay open) until 9 o'clock. 218

12. At least three people in the company Ed Reidinger, Gertrude Flanagan, and Hope Crawley have volunteered to donate O positive blood. 202 219

13. In about three months from now say, November 30 why don't we meet to review the committee's progress in drafting guidelines for an internal recycling program? 211a

14. Attached are the notes I made during each session at the management seminar (except the session on reducing employee absenteeism, which I missed.) 225a

15. Timothy Noonan, the head of our Chapel Hill North Carolina operations, may be taking over as manager of the Mount Vernon New York office. 219

16. Ella Garner—She used to work in your legal department, didn't she—has a good chance of being appointed a federal judge in the Ninth Circuit. 214b

Directions: Supply missing punctuation and strike out or correct any inappropriate punctuation in the following sentences. Change the capitalization as necessary. Circle all changes you make. **References:** ¶¶227–299 (primarily on quotation marks and the use of italics or underlining).

17. All he would say to the reporters was "I have no comment to make at this time

256a
247a

18. Please forward any mail marked "Personal" otherwise, hold everything else until I return to the office.

248a

19. What was the meaning you intended to convey in the phrase "must be completed within a reasonable time?"

249b

20. I think you ought to read Chapter 5, Managing Your Problem-Solving Time in Right on Time!: The Complete Guide for Time-Pressured Managers.

242
247a
289a

21. I've been given <u>carte</u> <u>blanche</u> on the design and packaging of our new cologne.

287

22. All personnel evaluation memos must be labeled "Confidential"

247a

23. All Beverly would say was this "If you want to get to the bottom of the matter, why don't you ask Terry"

256b
249a
256a

24. Why would Gina say, "I'm going to start updating my résumé."

257

25. The term infer means to draw a conclusion from someone else's words or actions; the term imply means to suggest something by your own words or actions.

286
248a
247a

26. "How will we explain this decision to the shareholders?," I asked.

254

27. How did you like Hank's latest article, "Are Happy Days Really Here Again?"?

258

28. In her memo of June 3 Hazel says, "I'll keep you appraised (sic) of our progress in improving language skills throughout the organization."

283
296a

29. The real question is, "Should we be expanding into areas where we have no in-house expertise?"

229

30. Altschuler's speech to the financial analysts was well received. (His later comments to the press (see the December 13 issue of "The Wall Street Journal") created quite an uproar, I understand.)

296b
289a

31. How many of our employees have read <u>The Art of Getting Things Done</u>?

290a

32. What this company needs is an "ombudsman," someone who would represent our customers' interests and make sure that their complaints were fairly resolved.

287

33. Harry Halpin, the noted financial analyst, says, "In my experience . . . . these short-term fluctuations in stock prices mean nothing."

274

34. Here are the procedures one authority recommends for typing messages on postcards:
   "First, set the left and right margins at 0.5 inch."
   "Next, type the date on the third line from the top of the card, beginning at the center.
   Omit the name and address of the person to whom the card is being sent.

265b

35. "I would like to urge you all" said the speaker, Nancy Ellington, to read an article entitled "The Salvation of Our Cities" in this month's issue of The Atlantic."

262
245a
289a

7

Editing Survey A

Directions: Supply missing punctuation and strike out or correct any inappropriate punctuation in the following **personal letter.** Change the capitalization as necessary. Circle all changes you make. **References:** Sections 1–2.

Dear Mark: **1**

When you came to visit last Sunday with Sally and the kids you were obviously brooding about **2**
your "dead-end job as a corporate accountant". Yesterday, I came across an article in <u>The New</u> **3**
<u>York Times</u> that might provide the solution to your problem. (I seem to have mislaid the article **4**
but I'll send it along, as soon as it turns up. **5**

Have you considered becoming a CMA. "What's that," I hear you asking? Well you know that **6**
a CPA is a certified public accountant — someone who 1) works for a variety of clients and 2) has **7**
passed a number of required courses and exams administered by the American Institute of **8**
Certified Public Accountants. To become a CMA you have to work within a corporation, have at **9**
least two years of managerial accounting experience and meet all the certification requirements of **10**
the Institute of Management Accountants. **11**

"Big deal" I can hear you thinking. Why bother?" According to the article, (which has to be **12**
around here somewhere top corporate executives are looking for management accountants, who **13**
can play a bigger part in shaping corporate strategies in an age of intensified global competition, **14**
and rapid technological changes. Because these top executives recognize the value of certification, **15**
corporate accountants with a CMA rating are more likely to get the higher-level, management **16**
accounting jobs. Moreover the CMA designation typically commands a higher salary, for example, **17**
CMAs in your age group (30–39) earn about $10,000 more than people with the same experience **18**
but without the certification. **19**

If you want to follow up on this idea, the Institute of Management Accountants is located at: **20**
10 Paragon Drive, Montvale NJ 07645, the phone number is 800-638-4427. If you're not **21**
interested, just pitch this letter in the nearest circular file. Which is where all of your father's **22**
brilliant ideas typically wind up. I really don't care as a matter of fact what happens to your career. **23**
It's my grandchildren's future that I worry about. Give them all a hug for me. **24**

Name _____ Date _____ Class _____ 15

Directions: Supply missing punctuation and strike out or correct any inappropriate punctuation in the following **personal letter.** Change the capitalization as necessary. Circle all changes you make. **References:** Sections 1–2.

Dear Mary Lee,   **1**

     You've been working much too hard lately, don't you think. I'd like to propose a three-day   **2**

getaway for the two of us—and maybe our husbands as well. The occasion? A conference   **3**

sponsored by the North Carolina Bed & Breakfast Association. Friends of ours—Barbara and Gerry   **4**

Ryan tell me that the conference is designed to appeal not only to <u>perspiring</u> innkeepers (those   **5**

who are currently doing it) and <u>expiring</u> innkeepers (those who want to get out from under) but   **6**

also to <u>aspiring</u> innkeepers (namely you and me.) The conference formally begins on Saturday,   **7**

February 24 at 4 p.m., and it runs until 12:30 p.m. on Monday, the 26th. If we register for only   **8**

one day's series of meetings the fee is $75; for all three days $125.   **9**

     It sounds a little crazy I know but you and I are always talking about how much fun it would   **10**

be to move away from Washington D.C. and set ourselves up as country innkeepers. Even if the   **11**

idea is only a pipe dream right now, and can't be seriously pursued for another thirty years, it   **12**

would still be a lot of fun to find out what's involved from people who really know.   **13**

     The location of the conference alone makes the trip worthwhile—the Biltmore Estate in   **14**

Asheville, North Carolina. The Biltmore House itself is a national treasure I'm told. Commissioned   **15**

in 1887 by George Vanderbilt and modeled after elegant French chateaus it remains the largest,   **16**

private home in this country today, with its 35 guest rooms, its banquet hall and library, its   **17**

handsome collection of sculpture and paintings and its extensive grounds. It will take us from six   **18**

to eight hours to get there depending on which of us does most of the driving.   **19**

     All the meetings will be held right on the grounds of the estate but there will be time each   **20**

day to work in as much exploring and sightseeing as we like. It may help you to know that, if we   **21**

register by January 15, we can be sure of getting attractive accommodations at one of the local   **22**

inns. For only $50 a night.   **23**

     The conference offers formal presentations on virtually every topic you can think of. (For   **24**

example the title of one speech is How to Handle Difficult Guests). One especially nice feature of   **25**

the program Mary Lee is all the time set aside for networking. In that way we can talk with some   **26**

of the perspiring innkeepers, the ones who know what it's all about, moreover, we can meet some   **27**

of the expiring innkeepers, the ones who might have just the place you'd love to take over.   **28**

     One final thought. Why don't you persuade your husband, Jeff, to make the trip with you. If   **29**

he says "yes," I'm sure I could get Dave to come, too. The only question is how can you resist so   **30**

attractive a proposition. Look why don't you talk this over with Jeff and get back to me? The   **31**

sooner I get a positive response from you the faster I can make all the necessary arrangements.   **32**

8 Capitalization

Directions: If the boldface word or phrase is correctly capitalized, write C in the answer column. If not, correct it as follows: To change a capital letter to a small letter, draw a line through it (The). To change a small letter to a capital letter, draw three lines under it (the). Circle all changes you make. **References:** ¶¶301–330.

1.	Have you found the Pelikan **company** to be a dependable supplier?	1. _____	309a 320a
2.	Let's meet in the lobby of the **hotel** and then go on to the convention.	2. _____	308
3.	**Attorney general** Harriet Cox has not yet issued an opinion.	3. _____	312a
4.	While you're in Washington, get a reaction from several **senators.**	4. _____	307 314
5.	My **uncle** gave me his medical library when he closed his practice.	5. _____	319a
6.	Please ask the **legal department** to review the attached letter of agreement.	6. _____	322
7.	That legislation was passed in 1986 by the **Ninety-Ninth Congress.**	7. _____	325
8.	I seriously question whether the proposed bill is **constitutional.**	8. _____	304
9.	Do you think the **governor** will support the antipollution measure?	9. _____	313b
10.	Our new offices are at the corner of Wilson and Sixth **streets.**	10. _____	309a
11.	I have applied for a fellowship at the **University Of The South.**	11. _____	303 320
12.	Our aim is to set up a franchised operation in every state in the **union.**	12. _____	330a
13.	How do you plan to increase revenues, **governor,** without raising taxes?	13. _____	315
14.	The people in **accounting** want us to cut 15 percent from our budgets.	14. _____	323
15.	Should the chapter numbers go in **Roman** numerals or be spelled out?	15. _____	306
16.	I think we ought to submit a bid on the **van Vleck** property along the river.	16. _____	311e
17.	The **president** of Benjamin Brothers has announced his resignation.	17. _____	313d
18.	I would like some more information about the **company's** health plan.	18. _____	321
19.	All **Federal** and state funding for this training program will end on June 30.	19. _____	328
20.	The flower garden was sponsored by the Belmont **chamber of commerce.**	20. _____	309a 320a
21.	Do you still have an opening for a **Systems Analyst?**	21. _____	313e
22.	The remaining question is, **how** will this new program be funded?	22. _____	301d
23.	Attending the conference was Watertown's **mayor,** Gilbert Kohlman.	23. _____	312b
24.	We had the premises inspected by someone from our local **Fire Department.**	24. _____	327
25.	How do you think **Senator-Elect** Coghill will vote on the bond issue?	25. _____	317
26.	There has been some talk about an antitrust action by the **Federal Government.**	26. _____	329
27.	Noel Byrd, **Vice President** of Milex Labs, will testify at an FDA hearing.	27. _____	313d
28.	A detailed analysis of the responses to our survey is given in Appendix A (**See** pages 216–224).	28. _____	302a
29.	The massive murals in the Metropolitan Opera House were done by **Painter** Marc Chagall.	29. _____	312c
30.	Someone in their **Accounting Department** should be able to explain.	30. _____	322

Directions: Correct the capitalization in the following sentences. If a sentence is correctly capitalized, write *C* in the answer column. Circle all changes you make. **References:** ¶¶301–330.

31. Ms. Eileen Kilmer, Executive Vice President of the Hampton real estate agency, says, "real estate prices are expected to remain stable for the rest of the year."

31. _____ 313d 309a 320a 301c

32. The current Mayor, Walter Marx, will honor Former Mayor George Gille and Mayor-Elect William Pavlick at a reception.

32. _____ 312b 317

33. *In a company memo:* Janet Russo, Manager of the human resources department, has been named head of the equal employment opportunity committee.

33. _____ 313d 322

34. This conflict between the U.S. department of the treasury and the federal reserve board dates back to the days of the Roosevelt administration. Although the board has brought the matter before the supreme court, the court feels that this is an administrative rather than a Constitutional issue.

34. _____ 325 328 326 304

35. Leaders from both the republican and the democratic parties met today with the president at the white house. An announcement from the oval office will be sent shortly to the senate and the house.

35. _____ 309a 313b 305 326 313d

36. Dr. Wanda A. Jory, Research Director for Biogenetic labs, will be an adjunct professor at our local University for the coming academic year.

36. _____ 309a 320a 308 313e

37. I would like to apply for the job of Regional Manager in your sales department.

37. _____ 322

38. Your Uncle, John Traynor, was identified in *the Wall Street Journal* as the person behind the du Hamel takeover attempt.

38. _____ 319a 324a 311e

39. *From a city agency's memo:* The mayor and the city council will meet tomorrow to discuss the Garvey company's application to construct a Shopping Mall on the block bounded by Summer, Marsh, Oak, and Maple streets.

39. _____ 313c 327 307 309a

40. When Radical Author William Boynton accepted a two-year grant from the Huntington foundation, reporters asked this question: "Tell us, Sir, how does it feel to be supported by the establishment?"

40. _____ 312c 309a 315 305

41. *From the Whitlock University course catalog:* The university offers a wide variety of courses to first-year students. However, for course titles marked with an asterisk, please get the approval of the Department Head before signing up.

41. _____ 321 308

42. *From an educational journal:* Whitlock University has announced plans to establish a Medical School in the next three years. Details of the University's plans were released today by the President.

42. _____ 307 321 313d

43. I want to apologize for the problems you had with our credit department. According to Ms. Marie Longo, the Manager of the Department, you now have a credit balance of $78.10.

43. _____ 322 313d 321

9

Capitalization (Continued)

Directions: If the boldface word or phrase is correctly capitalized, write *C* in the answer column. If not, correct it as follows: To change a capital letter to a small letter, draw a line through it *T̷he*. To change a small letter to a capital letter, draw three lines under it *t̲h̲e̲*. Circle all changes you make. **References:** ¶¶331–366.

1. My investment portfolio is managed by a Manhattan brokerage house that has excellent contacts on the **Street.**   1. _____ 332

2. Our business is targeted chiefly at the **Winter** tourist trade.   2. _____ 343

3. Please read **"Sales Tax is Sure to be Reduced"** in today's newspaper.   3. _____ 360

4. I used to stay at the Melrose Hotel, but the **Hotel** has gone downhill recently.   4. _____ 331

5. Will we need a special charter to do business in the **State** of Georgia?   5. _____ 335a

6. What undergraduate courses does the university offer in the area of **Western Civilization?**   6. _____ 340 352

7. In the late **nineties** we had to shift our business to new product lines.   7. _____ 345

8. You can quickly find the names of other suppliers in the **yellow pages.**   8. _____ 356a

9. I'm still not happy with the wording in **Paragraph** 3.   9. _____ 359

10. Bud's living in the **bay area,** but I can't tell you precisely where.   10. _____ 333a

11. No **midwesterner** would know what you meant by an "egg cream."   11. _____ 339

12. Ted's promotion is a perfect illustration of the Peter **principle.**   12. _____ 346

13. At times like this, we could use a crash course in the **ten commandments.**   13. _____ 350a

14. Please be sure to give your **social security** number along with your name.   14. _____ 347a

15. I grew up in Ripley, a small town in **Western** Tennessee north of Memphis.   15. _____ 341

16. When do you think the **City** of Clifton will change its zoning laws?   16. _____ 334

17. This year we will work only a half day on Christmas **eve.**   17. _____ 342

18. I remained in Santa Fe when my parents moved back **east.**   18. _____ 338

19. I expect to receive my **Master's** degree next spring.   19. _____ 353

20. *In a contract:* Roger L. Bork, hereinafter called the **buyer,** agrees to . . .   20. _____ 358

21. My father foresaw the boom in residential real estate after **World War II.**   21. _____ 344a

22. We'll be touring **northern** Vermont for much of our vacation.   22. _____ 341

23. *In an advertisement:* Try Northridge's **All-Natural Wheat Bread** for a treat.   23. _____ 355 357

24. Mrs. Fry said in her letter that she did not pretend to speak for all **Blacks.**   24. _____ 348a

25. Our daughter Ellen is doing her **Junior** year of college abroad.   25. _____ 354

26. *In a heading:* Twentieth-**century** Achievements in Civil Rights   26. _____ 363

27. I'm taking courses in English **Literature** in a special weekend program.   27. _____ 352

28. Mr. van Lieuw was originally a native of **the** Netherlands.   28. _____ 337a

29. I just put my faith in the Lord and let **him** work things out for me.   29. _____ 349b

30. Under separate cover I'm sending you a copy of **Growing up at Last.**   30. _____ 360a 361c

Directions: Correct the capitalization in the following sentences. If a sentence is correctly capitalized, write *C* in the answer column. Circle all changes you make. **References:** ¶¶301–366.

31. My family down south can't understand how I can enjoy living in the big Apple. Wait till they see my apartment in the village.

31. _____
338
333a
332

32. I will check with American airlines at Kennedy airport to see whether anyone has turned in the Manila envelope you lost.

32. _____
309a
331
306

33. You may get a laugh out of Ella's new article, "Nirvana is not as great a place as it's cracked up to be."

33. _____
360
361

34. The supporting data is presented in appendix 4. (See, in particular, chart 3 on page 514 and column 2 of table 14 on page 631.)

34. _____
359

35. Jennie Moore will be coming back east to serve as District Manager for all of New England plus the State of New York. All of her customers and business associates from the twin cities are going to miss her.

35. _____
338
313e
335a
333a
345

36. At the beginning of the Twentieth Century, my Grandfather moved out west and founded a small seed business. By the late Nineteen-thirties, just before the start of the second world war, the Company had annual sales of $3,000,000.

36. _____
319
338
345
344a
321

37. I am now a Senior at the university of Tennessee, majoring in Business Administration. I expect to get my Bachelor's degree this Spring.

37. _____
354
309a
352
353
343

38. The Mid-March reports indicate that sales are strong in the northeast but are faltering in the Farm Belt and the Sunbelt.

38. _____
363
338
333a

39. My brother-in-law works for the State as a Photographer in the department of travel and tourism.

39. _____
335b
313e
325

40. I have asked the reverend Frank Carleo, Pastor of St. Mark's roman catholic church, to give the invocation at the Lions club banquet on veterans day.

40. _____
312a
313a
320a
309a
342

41. When Bart Peterson returns to the States this Spring, I will take over his job in the middle east.

41. _____
335a
343
338

42. We need stronger Environmental Protection Laws if we are to save the Earth from destructive pollution.

42. _____
346b
351

43. Wilma Cooley, the congresswoman from South Dakota, will head a house committee studying safety procedures in nuclear plants, especially those in earthquake-prone areas on the coast.

43. _____
313b
326
332

44. For our upcoming Computer Convention I think we ought to invite someone like Tracy Kidder as our keynote speaker. Among his impressive credentials is the fact that he won the Pulitzer prize for *The Soul Of A New Machine*.

44. _____
308
364
360a

10 Numbers

Directions: Circle all errors in number style, and write the correct forms in the answer column. Follow the **figure** style (¶¶401–403) unless another style is called for. If a sentence is correct as given, write *C* in the answer column. **References:** ¶¶401–428, 461, 465.

1. We'll be leaving in 8 days for a month's trip to Australia.
   1. _____ 401a

2. Last year we mailed 6 million fliers; this year, 8,000,000.
   2. _____ 403b / 461

3. I would like to respond to your letter dated May twenty-first.
   3. _____ 407b / 414

4. Our new van cost several $1000 dollars more than we had budgeted.
   4. _____ 423

5. Effective July 1, parkway tolls will be increased to 40¢.
   5. _____ 418

6. Nelson E. R. Dillon the third is forming his own law firm.
   6. _____ 426

7. I requisitioned 6 laptop computers but got approval to buy only two.
   7. _____ 402

8. The council consists of 11 Democrats, eight Republicans, and one independent.
   8. _____ 402 / 404a

9. *Word style:* We have invited 75 people to our daughter's wedding.
   9. _____ 465a

10. Please call the banquet manager and say we expect about 300 guests.
    10. _____ 401a

11. We will celebrate the company's 150th anniversary next month.
    11. _____ 424

12. *Word style:* Over 21 million TV viewers saw our show last night.
    12. _____ 404a / 465a-b

13. A really good attaché case can cost $150.00 or more.
    13. _____ 415

14. Eighty people out of 100 could not remember the advertiser's name.
    14. _____ 421 / 404a

15. *Word style:* Between 300 and 325 people responded to our ad.
    15. _____ 405

16. Pergola Industries stock was selling today at two dollars a share.
    16. _____ 413a

17. *Formal style:* We will arrive in Paris on the 6th of April.
    17. _____ 407a

18. *Emphatic style:* Our Summer Sale will run until the 1st of September.
    18. _____ 407a

19. The building will cost between $18 and $20 million to construct.
    19. _____ 416d

20. Nearly 2/3 of those surveyed preferred the package done in orange.
    20. _____ 427a

21. The warehouse expansion is scheduled to begin July 1st, 2006.
    21. _____ 408

22. The cost of gas is now three and a half times what it was in 1970.
    22. _____ 428a

23. The outside of the building has not been painted since June 2000.
    23. _____ 410

24. I found a printer who can do these brochures for only $.30 apiece.
    24. _____ 418a

25. 64 pages of the book contain full-color illustrations.
    25. _____ 421

26. Last year our sales were $3,574,119; this year we will do over $4 million.
    26. _____ 403b / 461a / 417

27. The owners of that office building have cut the price by $½ million.
    27. _____ 461

28. You may participate in the pension plan after your 30th birthday.
    28. _____ 424

Name _____ Date _____ Class _____

29. Our semiannual sales meeting starts on the 2d. of March.   29. _____ 407a 425a

30. Pay one-half of the balance now and the other half in six months.   30. _____ 427c

31. Fran can give you 100 reasons why the report is not yet completed.   31. _____ 401c

32. The variance is less than three-sixteenths of an inch.   32. _____ 427a

33. The pattern calls for 7-3/8 yards of material.   33. _____ 428b

34. Our chief competitor has just cut prices by ten percent.   34. _____ 401b

35. About ten to 15 callers mentioned the typo in last Sunday's ad.   35. _____ 402

36. *Word style:* Can your living room hold as many as 125 people?   36. _____ 404a

37. All I wanted was 50 cents worth of rubber bands.   37. _____ 418a

38. A good fax machine will run between $175 and 250.   38. _____ 419 427b

39. Four fifths of our orders come from just three states.   39. _____ 421

40. My bank statement shows a balance of only six dollars and 14 cents.   40. _____ 413a

Directions: Rewrite the following sentences to correct errors in number style and related punctuation. Follow the **figure** style unless another style is called for. **References:** ¶¶401–428, 461, 465.

41. We sold eight refrigerators, 11 stoves, and three freezers in only two days. _____

_____ 402

42. Thank you for your letter of May 9th, in which you asked about a deed dated 3/3/01. _____

_____ 407b 408c

43. On July 10, we will submit the will dated August 11th, 2004 for probate. _____

_____ 410 408d

44. Allow $750,000 to $1 million for expenses plus another $100 thousand for fees. _____

_____ 416c 461

45. The unit cost of $1.71 represents 56 cents for parts, 93¢ for labor, and $0.22 for shipping.

_____

_____ 418b

46. On the first of May, 2008 I promise to pay Six Thousand ($6000) Dollars . . . _____ 408 410 420a

_____

47. $325 seems to me to be a lot to charge for so small a repair job. _____

_____ 422

48. Join the 100s of voters in the 21st Ward who want to return Tim Bannigan for his 5th term in

Congress._____ 423 424

_____

49. In ¼ of an hour we can show you how to cut your packaging costs in ½. _____

_____ 427

40. *Word style:* On the 25th of September we expect more than 20,000 residents will help to

celebrate the 100th anniversary of the founding of the city. _____

_____ 407a 404a 427d

_____

11 Numbers (Continued)

Directions: Circle all errors in number style, and write the correct forms in the answer column. Follow the **figure** style (¶¶401–403) unless another style is called for. If a sentence is correct as given, write *C* in the answer column. **References:** ¶¶429–470 plus the basic rules (¶¶401–406).

1. Take Route I-95 to Exit 69, go north on Route 9 to the Essex turnoff, and then go west for three miles to Ivoryton.

    1. _____ 429a

2. Children who are not 5 years old by October 31 may not enter school this fall.

    2. _____ 433

3. A 48-month automobile loan might be easier for you to carry.

    3. _____ 436a

4. Why hasn't Bly & Bly reordered from us in the past 6 months?

    4. _____ 437

5. You can avoid the tunnel traffic if you leave home by 6 A.M.

    5. _____ 440a / 440b

6. If you order by August 15, take an extra five percent off the total.

    6. _____ 447a

7. Perhaps #78312 was voided and a new purchase order was issued.

    7. _____ 455

8. Our markets expanded dramatically between 1995–2005.

    8. _____ 459b

9. We are planning a first printing of 8000 copies.

    9. _____ 461a

10. Feel free to call me at home between 8:00 and 9:30 p.m.

    10. _____ 440c

11. The table on page 1,157 shows the properties of the tested alloys.

    11. _____ 462

12. *General style:* The reception room needs only a 9- × 12-foot rug.

    12. _____ 432

13. We plan to fly to Bermuda to celebrate our 25th wedding anniversary.

    13. _____ 435

14. Our capital needs were far simpler in the early 1990's.

    14. _____ 438 / 464

15. *Formal style:* The Ebert-Rogers reception will begin at 7 o'clock.

    15. _____ 441a

16. The council approved the tax increase by a vote of eight to two.

    16. _____ 451

17. There may be a 15–20° drop in temperature at night.

    17. _____ 453b

18. It's unheard of for someone in her early 30's to be made CEO.

    18. _____ 434

19. By the late 90's over half of our sales came from exports.

    19. _____ 439a

20. *Formal style:* The awards ceremony will begin at eight thirty.

    20. _____ 442a

21. In the markets we serve, women outnumber men on a ratio of 5 to 2.

    21. _____ 450a / 418c

22. *Footnote in catalog:* *Add fifty ¢ to cover the cost of handling.

    22. _____ 453a

23. *Footnote in a report:* *See pages 400–02.

    23. _____ 460b / 465b

24. I can trace my family back almost three-hundred years.

    24. _____ 437

25. To approximate our unit cost, divide the list price by 5.

    25. _____ 452

26. Let me give you my unlisted phone number—555/4989.

    26. _____ 454a

27. The year 2008 in roman numerals is MMVII.

    27. _____ 469 / 467

28. Maude is in her seventys, but she doesn't look more than sixty.

    28. _____ 434

29. *In an ad:* Salary up to $50K to qualified person with solid experience.

    29. _____ 470

30. During the summer the temperature rarely goes above the low 80's.

    30. _____ 464

Directions: Rewrite the following sentences to correct errors in number style and related punctuation. Follow the **figure** style unless another style is called for. **References:** ¶¶401–470.

31. I will be at the booth between 9:30 a.m. in the morning and 12 a.m. noon. _____
440h
440f

32. Mrs. Engle will get a finder's fee of $12000, or .5% of the price paid for the property. _____
461a
448a
401a

33. I have 2 questions about Invoice No. 10,414 dated May 3rd, 2007. _____
455a
463
408d

34. In 1999, seventy percent of our revenues came from only eighteen items in our product line.
456
447a
401a

35. 2,000 64-page booklets can be printed for about 90¢ each. _____
421
457
418a

36. From 2005–2008 we plan to do an intensive study of 8th-grade students. _____
459b
424

37. On January 1 2008 1 will be exactly 22 years, 4 months, and 7 days old. _____
410
433

38. I am five feet, five inches tall, and I weigh a hundred and forty-two pounds. _____
430
429a

39. Since 2003, an employee with more than twenty years of service can get full retirement

benefits at age sixty-two. _____
410
436a
433

40. On her 21st birthday Jane Best will inherit ¼ of a million dollars. _____
435
417

41. Back in the 90's it was easy to get a thirty-year mortgage at six and a half %. _____
439a
436a
448b
447a

42. I like to get to the office at 7 and leave early in the p.m. _____
442a
440d

43. *Formal style:* Let's meet on the 21st of June at 9:30 o'clock. _____
407a
441b

44. *In an ad:* All inventory must be sold! Enjoy 50–70% price reductions! _____
453b

45. Between 2005–2008 we plan to open three discount outlets in Ohio, one in Kentucky, and

twelve in Indiana. _____
459b
402

46. *Formal style:* Over 1500 guests danced till 2 a.m. o'clock at the University Club. _____
404a
466
440e

12

Abbreviations

Directions: Supply the correct abbreviation for each of the following terms. **References:** ¶¶501–550.

1.	Senior	506a 518	21.	doctor of philosophy	509 519a
2.	Corporation	520b 541	22.	personal computer	541 544a
3.	continued	505a 541	23.	that is	507 545
4.	vice president	541	24.	North Dakota	527 1334b
5.	Doctors	517a	25.	cubic centimeters	509 538e
6.	Company	520b 541	26.	fiscal year	504 541
7.	Wednesday	532	27.	kilogram	537a 541
8.	pounds	535a 541	28.	December	532
9.	liter	537a 541	29.	year to date	541
10.	end of month	541 542	30.	modulator and demodulator	522c
11.	chief operating officer	541	31.	not applicable	541
12.	bulletin board service	544a	32.	input/output	544a
13.	bachelor of laws	509 519a	33.	digital video disc	546
14.	Incorporated	520b 541	34.	facsimile	510
15.	United States	525	35.	[Jay Fenn] the third	518d
16.	south-southwest	531b	36.	and other people	545
17.	miles per hour	535a 541	37.	not in my backyard	522a
18.	kilometers per hour	538a 541	38.	Felicity R. O'Malley	516c
19.	for example	545	39.	random-access memory	544a
20.	postage and handling	541	40.	my eyes glaze over	522a

Directions: Underline any word or abbreviation that is incorrectly styled, and write the correct form in the answer column. If a sentence is correct, write *C* in the answer column. **References:** ¶¶501–550.

41.	When I next visit Mount Vernon, I hope to visit Doctor Cali.	41.	529a 517a
42.	How long will it take to drive from Sandpoint, Idaho, to Eugene, Ore.?	42.	504 526
43.	Samuel Potter Junior is expected to be named the new CEO.	43.	518a 541
44.	Attached are copies of the following purchase orders: Nos 61715, 63821, and 64111.	44.	506a 455
45.	We need another Wats line to handle the dramatic surge in orders.	45.	522a
46.	The best programming consultant I know is J. G. Head of Saint Louis.	46.	516a 529b

47. Either a tax lawyer or a C.P.A. could advise you on how to treat the proceeds of this sale for income tax purposes. **47.** _____ 519g 541

48. Next year we plan to open more discount outlets throughout the U.S. **48.** _____ 525

49. When the temperature reaches 30°C., you'll want a bathing suit, not an overcoat. **49.** _____ 537a 505b

50. How do you feel about a breakfast meeting at 7 oclock? **50.** _____ 533 508

51. I need to get ready for a tax audit by the I.R.S. **51.** _____ 524

52. Top management wants a Harvard MBA to critique our long-range plans. **52.** _____ 519b

53. Representatives from the Afl-Cio are now evaluating the impact of automation on employment levels. **53.** _____ 520a 527

54. Edna Helmstatter does liaison work for us in Washington, D.C. **54.** _____ 528a 544a

55. Sales of our CD-ROM products have increased 22 % this year. **55.** _____ 543d 505a

56. *Note at the bottom of a page:* Cont'd on next page. **56.** _____ 541

57. Would you be willing to serve on the ad. hoc. committee being set up to study alternative HMO plans? **57.** _____ 545 541 504

58. The morning session begins at 9:30 a.m.; the afternoon session, at 1:30 P.M. **58.** _____ 533 509

59. Bette Dorsey will receive her Ed. D. this spring. **59.** _____ 519a

60. The next meeting of the Alumni Club is scheduled for the 14th. of May. **60.** _____ 510

61. Why do our customers prefer Brand X. over our product line? **61.** _____ 547

62. Our uptown office is located at 4139 Burney Boulevard, SE. **62.** _____ 531a 543c

63. We should be doubling our investment in R & D if we expect to grow. **63.** _____ 546

64. Doctor Mark Duff, Ph.D., has been appointed to a federal advisory panel to study ways to boost the growth rate of our GDP. **64.** _____ 517a 519c 546

65. These relics must date back at least to 500 BC. **65.** _____ 508

Directions: Rewrite the following sentences to correct any errors in abbreviation style. **References:** ¶¶501–550.

66. Mr. Morton Li, MBA, CPA, is an expert on L.B.O. strategies. _____ 519c 519g 541

_____

67. The Hon. Frieda L. Goodman will speak tomorrow at 10 a.m. and at 3 o'clock. _____ 517e 504

_____ 515

68. Ask Ed. whether he thinks Mr. G wants to sell his condo. in L.A. _____ 516d 510 526

_____

69. Messers Amory and Powell have talked with L.B. Kelley about a partnership. _____ 517a 516a

_____ 517a

70. Mister Rudolfi has OK'd your trip to Ft. Worth. _____ 550 548 529a

_____

13 Editing Survey B

Directions: Edit the following material (a draft of a news release) for capitalization, number, and abbreviation style. Circle all changes you make. **References:** Sections 3–5; pages 358–359 or the inside back cover for proofreaders' marks.

Doctor Raymond Kaufman, President of Computer Concepts, Inc., has announced that on **1**
Sep. 1 Frederick de Winter, thirty-six, will join the company as Executive Vice President in **2**
charge of special projects. **3**

Mr. de Winter developed his passionate interest in computers over 30 years ago. During **4**
his Junior year at M.I.T., this brilliant software engineer achieved his first commercial success **5**
with a spreadsheet program, which he sold to a major software publisher for $100000 plus **6**
royalties. Following his graduation with a degree in Computer Science, this computer whiz **7**
devoted his newly won profits and his extraordinary talents to developing a machine that could **8**
scan printed material and convert it into synthesized speech for the blind. **9**

It is de Winter's extensive background in synthesized speech that brings him to Computer **10**
Concepts. Last Fall the Company announced plans to speed up its development of a voice-activated **11**
computer. Dragon Systems and Lernout & Hauspie have already developed software that can **12**
recognize 250,000 words and convert speech to text at a rate of one hundred sixty words a minute. **13**

The progress made by these companies has attracted the interest of industry giants like **14**
I.B.M. and A. T. & T. as well as smaller innovative firms. J.V. Terrant, the c.e.o. of Computer **15**
Concepts and an expert on C.A.D. (computer-aided design), says, "voice-activated computers repre- **16**
sent a potentially huge market in the U.S. Industry analysts estimate that sales could easily **17**
exceed $2,000,000,000." **18**

The field has already come a long way from its early beginnings. 15 years ago **19**
Parcel Services Of America was using a limited-vocabulary system that permitted workers to **20**
call out routing and sorting directions for each package without physically handling it. The **21**
latest software consists of continuous-speech recognition programs that allow you to dictate **22**
to your computer in a relatively natural manner (without having to pause between words). **23**
Yet the programs currently available have not yet achieved the 95% accuracy rate that **24**
experts consider a critical standard. And that is the challenge facing Computer Concepts. **25**

Fred de Winter recognizes the high risks entailed in his project, but he is eager to start **26**
work as soon as he transplants his family from the west coast. When interviewed at the **27**
Airport, he said, "My wife and I are excited about coming back east, and my 4 kids can't wait **28**
to experience their first Northern winter. If you think developing a voice-activated computer **29**
is a challenge, have you tried developing a voice-activated child?" **30**

Name _____ Date _____ Class _____ 27

Getting out the Vote: an Up-to-date Approach   **1**

My Grandfather recently recalled that when he was a young man, getting out the vote   **2**

usually meant that workers for each political machine went out and twisted a few arms. He   **3**

was reflecting on the fact that in the final decade of the Twentieth Century, the computer had   **4**

revolutionized the way politicians get people to vote for them.   **5**

Both the Republican and the Democratic parties are increasingly basing their strategies on   **6**

computer analyses. In a recent campaign for president, one election committee asked a computer   **7**

to match the names of all registered drivers against the names of all registered voters in a   **8**

particular State. The result was a list of unregistered voters, which was further analyzed so as   **9**

to identify those people most likely to vote for the Committee's candidate. The results on   **10**

election day were a dramatic vindication of this approach.   **11**

According to Pollster Norman Monagle of the Center For Public Research, "The election   **12**

game began to change in the Nineties. Candidates at all levels—Federal, state, and local—must   **13**

now find out all they can about the age, gender, and economic status of the voters." Even managers   **14**

of small-scale campaigns can now buy commercial software programs that sell for as little as   **15**

$75–100. (The cost of customized programs, of course, can run into the 1000's.)   **16**

The computer can do more than target unregistered voters. One candidate from the   **17**

Western part of Washington state, running for a seat in the house, learned from computer   **18**

analyses about a dramatic increase in the number of 18- to 24-year-olds and those over sixty in   **19**

his district. He immediately started to call on more schools and strengthen his support for those   **20**

on Social Security. As a result, he won by a substantial margin.   **21**

A Senator from the nutmeg state, running for election for the 2nd time, had access to a   **22**

computerized file of past speeches of her opponent. Once she publicly compared his past   **23**

positions and his current promises—especially on the Environmental Protection Law—you   **24**

wouldn't have given 2¢ for her opponent's chances.   **25**

A recent article, entitled "The Powerful Machine On The Political Scene," noted that the   **26**

computer would continue to effect massive changes in the conduct of our political campaigns,   **27**

changes that our founding fathers could never have foreseen. Nevertheless, even with the ready   **28**

accessibility of $75.00 software, the skills of political pros will always be needed. Even though   **29**

we advance further into the Computer Age, the conduct of politics will always be an art.   **30**

14

Plurals

Directions: Supply the correct plural form for each of the following items. **References:** ¶¶601–626; a dictionary (optional).

1.	area	_____	601	**31.**	address	_____ 602
2.	ability	_____	604	**32.**	day	_____ 605
3.	memo	_____	607a	**33.**	shelf	_____ 608b
4.	business	_____	602	**34.**	sketch	_____ 602
5.	belief	_____	608a	**35.**	company	_____ 604
6.	rule of thumb	_____	612a	**36.**	fee	_____ 601
7.	phenomenon	_____	614	**37.**	trade-off	_____ 612b
8.	criticism	_____	601	**38.**	stereo	_____ 606
9.	printout	_____	611	**39.**	woman	_____ 609
10.	agency	_____	604	**40.**	alumnus	_____ 614
11.	crash	_____	602	**41.**	Mr. and Mrs. Gaines	the _____ 615b
12.	Mr. and Mrs. Duffy	the _____	615c	**42.**	contract	_____ 601
13.	highway	_____	605	**43.**	boy	_____ 605
14.	foot	_____	609	**44.**	t	_____ 623 / 604
15.	vol.	_____	619	**45.**	photocopy	_____ 611
16.	byte	_____	601	**46.**	two	_____ 624b
17.	hang-up	_____	612b	**47.**	property	_____ 604
18.	apology	_____	604	**48.**	customer	_____ 601
19.	portfolio	_____	606	**49.**	echo	_____ 607b
20.	child	_____	610	**50.**	traveler's check	_____ 612d
21.	CEO	_____	622a	**51.**	graffito	_____ 614
22.	pro and con	_____	625	**52.**	witness	_____ 602
23.	tax	_____	602	**53.**	M.D.	_____ 622a
24.	taxi	_____	601	**54.**	Mr. and Mrs. Heinz	the _____ 615b
25.	index *(of a book)*	_____	614	**55.**	runner-up	_____ 612a
26.	X	_____	622a	**56.**	attorney	_____ 605
27.	inquiry	_____	604	**57.**	lb	_____ 620
28.	the German	the _____	617a	**58.**	Mr. and Mrs. Caro	the _____ 615a
29.	1990	_____	624a	**59.**	basis	_____ 614
30.	menu	_____	601	**60.**	fallacy	_____ 604

Name _____ Date _____ Class _____

Directions: Underline any word that is misspelled or misused, and write the correct form in the answer column. If a sentence is correct, write *C* in the answer column. **References:** ¶¶601–626; a dictionary (optional).

#	Sentence	Answer	Ref
61.	In selecting projects, he has only one criteria: profit.	61. _____	614
62.	Have the Weaver's moved out of the area?	62. _____	615a
63.	Let's get bids from three or four studioes before we decide.	63. _____	606
64.	Hal likes to flash a wad of twentys and fifties.	64. _____	624b
65.	Attached is a list of do's and don't's for the newcomers.	65. _____	625
66.	The Miss Perry are the sole heirs to their mother's estate.	66. _____	618b
67.	The two Terrys in our office keep getting each other's calls.	67. _____	616
68.	I have had no response to the six faxs I sent to Ted.	68. _____	602
69.	These drawings could become collectors' items in a few years.	69. _____	612d
70.	My sister-in-laws will help me with the painting.	70. _____	612a
71.	Please give my best regards to the McNeelys and the Welchs.	71. _____	615b
72.	Economists are now analyzing the effects of globalization on international markets throughout the 1990s.	72. _____	624a
73.	We're looking for men and woman with financial backgrounds.	73. _____	609
74.	As a result of the environmental damage, the company now faces a crises of confidence as well as numerous lawsuits.	74. _____	614
75.	All those editor in chiefs have rejected my manuscript.	75. _____	612a
76.	Let's invite the Farleys, the McCoys, and the Tullys.	76. _____	615c
77.	It's hard to distinguish the *n*'s and *u*'s in his handwriting.	77. _____	623
78.	Our attornies will send you a revised draft of the contract.	78. _____	605
79.	How soon can I get an analyses of our quarterly sales?	79. _____	614
80.	Please make two photocopies of the attached bill of ladings.	80. _____	611 / 612a
81.	We hope to attract new customers from outlying communitys.	81. _____	604
82.	The supporting data is given in Appendix B (see p. 48–52).	82. _____	621
83.	Our Februarys and Marchs are slow months as a rule.	83. _____	617a
84.	I am looking for results, not alibies.	84. _____	601
85.	Our wifes have opened a real estate agency in Mill Valley.	85. _____	608b
86.	He offered the cashier two handfuls of pennies.	86. _____	613
87.	I have always considered myself a loyal alumni of Duke.	87. _____	614
88.	Have the Romeroes returned their proxies?	88. _____	615a / 604
89.	We must devise more effective marketing strategys.	89. _____	604
90.	Their field staff consists only of Ph.D.s.	90. _____	622a
91.	Mme. Lenard and Tremont will oversee the arrangements.	91. _____	618
92.	How many new Macintosh's have been requisitioned?	92. _____	617a
93.	Four agencys are competing for the Longyear account.	93. _____	604
94.	The feetprint outside the window prove there were two thieves.	94. _____	611
95.	We have retained Messrs. Fina and Sternhagen to represent us.	95. _____	618

15

Possessives

Directions: For each singular noun in the first column, supply the correct forms for the singular possessive, the plural, and the plural possessive. **References:** ¶¶630–638 for possessive forms; ¶¶601–626 for plural forms.

SINGULAR	SINGULAR POSSESSIVE	PLURAL	PLURAL POSSESSIVE
1. contractor	630a	601	632a
2. boss	631a	602	632a
3. Hirsch	631a	the 615b	the 632a
4. attorney	630a	605	632a
5. child	630a	610	633
6. Columbo	630a	the 615a	the 632a
7. lady	630a	604	632a
8. file clerk	634	612a	635a
9. woman	630a	609	633
10. Koontz	631a	the 615b	the 632a
11. wife	630a	608b	632a
12. son-in-law	634	612a	635b
13. shareholder	634	611	635a
14. alumna	630a	614	633
15. Willis	631a	the 615b	the 632a
16. hero	630a	607b	632a
17. Kennedy	630a	the 615c	the 632a
18. CPA	638	622	638
19. emcee	630a	623	632a
20. secretary	630a	604	632a

Directions: Underline all errors and write the correct forms in the answer column. If a sentence is correct, write *C* in the answer column. **References:** ¶¶627–652.

21. Some changes in worker's compensation laws may be enacted this year.	21.	652 629
22. Mary Jo is applying for a six month's leave of absence.	22.	646
23. They seem to have no respect for one anothers' viewpoint.	23.	637
24. The alumnis' contributions to the Centennial Fund are 13 percent ahead of last year's figure.	24.	633
25. It's hard to manage two boss's correspondence at the same time.	25.	632 633

Name _____ Date _____ Class _____ 31

26. Anyone on Mrs. Adam's staff can handle that kind of problem.

26. _____ 631c

27. Our division's sale's goal for the year is $3.2 million.

27. _____ 628a

28. The green binders are mine; the red binders are her's.

28. _____ 636

29. Two CPA's audits have turned up no evidence of fraud.

29. _____ 638

30. Look for special discounts this month at your dealer.

30. _____ 644

31. Lida Wolfe has had fifteen years experience in the office automation industry.

31. _____ 629 646

32. The job offer depends on him being willing to travel.

32. _____ 647

33. Do you know John and Kathy's birthdays?

33. _____ 642a

34. You will need a vice presidents' signature on this invoice.

34. _____ 634

35. We plan to enter the childrens' wear market next fall.

35. _____ 633

36. Did you know that your favorite bakery has just lost it's lease?

36. _____ 636 633

37. The scholarship was given by the Womens' Union Club.

37. _____ 640a

38. Were you impressed with Frank Parker Jr.'s new partner?

38. _____ 639

39. Was there a witness to Ellis's and Marsh's contract?

39. _____ 643a

40. What did you think of our hostess' comments last night about her guest of honor?

40. _____ 631a

41. We've been invited to the Fergusons after the banquet.

41. _____ 644

42. All manager's travel plans may be curtailed for two months.

42. _____ 632

43. My surgeon was a college roommate of my wife.

43. _____ 648 632

44. Two dollars worth of oil could have prevented the problem.

44. _____ 646

45. I have to admit that their catalog looks a lot nicer than our's.

45. _____ 636 633

46. Next year the separate men and women's tournaments will be combined.

46. _____ 642a

Directions: Rewrite the following sentences to remove all errors and awkward expressions. **References:** ¶¶627–652.

47. I'm reluctant to put more money in my brothers-in-law's business. _____

_____ 635b

48. It was Wendy Donnelly, my lawyer's idea to insert that clause. _____

_____ 641

49. This quarter's inventory turnover rate is much better than last quarter. _____

_____ 644a

50. You'll find the quotation in the article's last paragraph. _____

_____ 645

51. A friend of mine's sister has just joined our firm as a partner. _____

_____ 648c

52. The new ad grew out of the product manager's nine-year-old daughter's sketch. _____

_____ 649

16 Spelling

Directions: In the answer column write the correct form of each word given in parentheses. **References:** ¶¶701–711; a dictionary (optional).

1. We are now (ship + ing) over 2000 units a day.
2. They have not yet tracked down the missing (ship + ment).
3. I gather Frank was (offer + ed) the West Coast opening.
4. Bart (refer + ed) to an earlier letter that I had never seen.
5. Feel free to give my name as a (refer + ence).
6. Sybil and I were shocked when the waiter (total + ed) our bill.
7. How has Kitchens Inc. (maintain + ed) so high a rate of growth?
8. I am currently (manage + ing) a retail jewelry store.
9. This decision has to be approved by higher (manage + ment).
10. Please record your (mile + age) and any expenses for gas.
11. You used superb (judge + ment) in answering Roy's complaint.
12. We need to probe into the (underlie + ing) causes.
13. I have tried and will go on (try + ing) to get some response.
14. You (display + ed) remarkable poise when you were challenged at the board meeting.
15. I (cancel + ed) the order on the basis of the first sample.
16. My assistant will be (record + ing) all the sessions.
17. Do you think these new regulations will be (enforce + able)?
18. We need a consultant with a (program + ing) background.
19. (Equip + ing) a new research lab will not be cheap.
20. Was Palmer (full + ly) aware of your feelings?

1. _____ 701
2. _____ 703
3. _____ 704
4. _____ 702
5. _____ 702
6. _____ 704
7. _____ 705
8. _____ 707a
9. _____ 708
10. _____ 707a
11. _____ 708
12. _____ 709
13. _____ 710a
14. _____ 711
15. _____ 704
16. _____ 706
17. _____ 707c
18. _____ 704
19. _____ 705
20. _____ 706

Directions: Select the correct form in parentheses, and write your answer in the column at the right. **References:** ¶¶712–718; a dictionary (optional).

21. Property owners are hoping for some tax (releif, relief) soon.
22. You need to adopt a more (flexable, flexible) position.
23. We have to become less (dependant, dependent) on our domestic markets and give new emphasis to exports.
24. The Fox project is (proceding, proceeding) on schedule.
25. Our research director will (analize, analyze) the government study and will report to the committee.
26. We have (received, recieved) over 250 answers to our ad.

21. _____ 712
22. _____ 713b
23. _____ 714
24. _____ 716b
25. _____ 715c
26. _____ 712

Name _____ Date _____ Class _____ 33

27. This memo (supercedes, supersedes) my earlier memo of May 4.   27. _____ 716a
28. We had strong (resistance, resistence) to our price increases.   28. _____ 714
29. Baldwin does not (weild, wield) as much power as he thinks.   29. _____ 712
30. Could you please submit two copies of your (resumé, résumé).   30. _____ 718a
31. This complaint is only an isolated (occurance, occurrence).   31. _____ 714
32. I do not think we should (intercede, interceed) in their dispute.   32. _____ 716c
33. Ms. Karras is now (supervising, supervizing) a staff of twelve.   33. _____ 715b
34. Is it (possable, possible) that Powers never saw the memo?   34. _____ 713b
35. The acquisition rumors are making everyone (panicy, panicky).   35. _____ 717

Directions: If the boldface word is correct as given, write *C* in the answer column. If the word is misspelled, supply the correct form. References: ¶¶719–720.

36. If you want to win Julie over, you need to take a different **tack.**   36. _____ 719
37. Please prepare a **seperate** memo of agreement for Mrs. Carey.   37. _____ 720
38. Negotiations have now broken down and are at an **impass.**   38. _____ 720
39. A corner office is one of the **prerequisites** of the CEO's job.   39. _____ 719
40. If you ask about the Taiwan incident, please be **discreet.**   40. _____ 719
41. Use the Farraday contract or something **similiar** as a model.   41. _____ 720
42. Your analysis is based on a number of **erronious** assumptions.   42. _____ 720
43. We can **accomodate** over 200 people in our meeting room.   43. _____ 720
44. I'm enclosing a copy of Mrs. Fonseca's **itinery.**   44. _____ 720
45. If Joe continues to **flaunt** the rules, he'll lose his job.   45. _____ 719
46. An analysis of last year's performance is due on **Febuary** 1.   46. _____ 720
47. According to our **personal** policy, you are entitled to two weeks' vacation after one year's employment.   47. _____ 719
48. I will have to **forego** your kind invitation to the theater.   48. _____ 719
49. We were given gold pins as a **momento** of the occasion.   49. _____ 720
50. Here's an **uninterested** appraisal of your investment portfolio.   50. _____ 719
51. **Basicly,** it is your unreasonable deadlines that are the problem.   51. _____ 720
52. It's hard to **guage** Marge's true feelings about the move.   52. _____ 720
53. When can we expect a **definate** answer from Ms. Russo?   53. _____ 720
54. Mr. Daumier has promised to **appraise** us of any new developments in the Busoni investigation.   54. _____ 719
55. This pamphlet will **aquaint** you with our discount policy.   55. _____ 720
56. How could such a **collossal** error get through undetected?   56. _____ 720
57. Kim's contribution to the success of the project was **miniscule.**   57. _____ 720
58. We need someone to act as **liasion** between the two committees.   58. _____ 720
59. Does Mark have the **temperment** to manage a staff of ten?   59. _____ 720
60. Thank you for responding so promptly to our **questionaire.**   60. _____ 720

34

17 Choosing the Right Word

Directions: Select the correct form in parentheses, and write your answer in the column at the right. **References:** ¶719.

1. How could these funds have been (disbursed, dispersed) without your okay?   1. _____

2. It (may be, maybe) too late to prevent the loss of the Rexford account.   2. _____

3. I could (cite, sight, site) numerous precedents for the court's ruling.   3. _____

4. Mrs. Campo played the (principal, principle) role in the negotiations.   4. _____

5. Please sign the (waver, waiver) of liability for your child's field trip.   5. _____

6. Your policy makes you (liable, libel) for the first $500 in damages.   6. _____

7. Our TV campaign has (peaked, piqued) the interest of many buyers.   7. _____

8. I'll be happy to write the (foreword, forward) for your book.   8. _____

9. The paint must be (especially, specially) mixed to match this chip.   9. _____

10. I refuse to (accede, exceed) to the board's demands.   10. _____

11. Many weeks have (passed, past) since you promised to write to us.   11. _____

12. The uproar at yesterday's meeting didn't (faze, phase) me a bit.   12. _____

13. We need to fight our competitors with all our (might, mite).   13. _____

14. The actual figures don't (gibe, jibe) with the earlier estimates.   14. _____

15. I will not comment out of (deference, difference) to Mrs. Cabot's views.   15. _____

16. We can invalidate the contract on the grounds of (undo, undue) influence.   16. _____

17. Cost overruns forced us to (expand, expend) more than we budgeted.   17. _____

18. Thanks (a lot, allot, alot) for all your help.   18. _____

19. These trays would (complement, compliment) your existing product line.   19. _____

20. With the latest financial setback, bankruptcy is (eminent, imminent).   20. _____

21. How can we (assure, ensure, insure) that the mistake will not recur?   21. _____

22. Our only recourse will be to get a (lean, lien) on his property.   22. _____

23. I am not (adverse, averse) to your getting a larger share of the profits.   23. _____

24. How can we (affect, effect) the reorganization with minimum confusion?   24. _____

25. Let's (adapt, adopt) the existing procedures rather than set up new ones.   25. _____

26. We (cannot, can not) only sell you new photocopiers but also service the ones you have.   26. _____

27. You must find some way to (brake, break) the sudden drop in sales.   27. _____

28. Are you free on Monday to meet with a (perspective, prospective) buyer?   28. _____

29. If you need help, Carole can (council, counsel, consul) you.   29. _____

30. We plan to appeal the decision rather than (accept, except) it.   30. _____

Name _____ Date _____ Class _____   35

Directions: Underline every word that is misspelled or misused, and write the correct form in the answer column. If a sentence is correct, write *C* in the answer column. **References:** ¶¶719–720; a dictionary (optional).

31. There were a number of errors and ommissions in the minutes.

31. _____ 720

32. In what catagory should I record these miscellaneous sales?

32. _____ 720

33. Waxman's presentation was amateurish and embarassing.

33. _____ 720

34. Our attorney believes that a complaint should be formerly lodged.

34. _____ 719

35. Ashberry's bankruptcy could put our own financial stability in jepardy.

35. _____ 720

36. We must insist on strict temperture controls in the laboratory.

36. _____ 720

37. Jon views each aquisition like a connoisseur eyeing a work of art.

37. _____ 720

38. It's your perogative to demand better liaison between the two groups.

38. _____ 720

39. Curtesy produces loyal customers and yields repeat business.

39. _____ 719

40. It was the consensus of the group that you proceed with your plan.

40. _____ 720

41. Mediocre products are never the bargins they are made out to be.

41. _____ 720

42. The alledged damage to the environment has been exaggerated.

42. _____ 720

43. Fewer then forty customers have returned our questionnaire.

43. _____ 719

44. You'll find a parking lot ajacent to our main entrance.

44. _____ 720

45. We'll have to forgo the priviledge of hearing you speak.

45. _____ 720

46. The only way to elimanate the deficit is to cut back on spending.

46. _____ 720

47. The directors will be arriving on the eighth or nineth of May.

47. _____ 720

48. This policy does not supersede anyone of the existing policies.

48. _____ 719

49. We've had phenominal success in launching this year's models.

49. _____ 720

50. We need to issue a corporate policy statement on sexual harrassment.

50. _____ 720

51. Making prophecies about the bond market is not exactly my forte.

51. _____ 719

52. Will government regulation be a help or a hinderance in this case?

52. _____ 720

53. Can you name any uninterested parties to serve as arbiters?

53. _____ 719

54. I implied from what you said that I would not be affected.

54. _____ 719

55. Why do I always mispell the word *grammar?*

55. _____ 720

56. Judge Frazier is an imminent jurist, renowned for her legal opinions.

56. _____ 719

57. The only way out of the dillemma is to waive your rights.

57. _____ 720

58. We can offer you a discount of 10 to 40 percent, depending on the quanity you order.

58. _____ 720

59. Frankly, I'm loathe to sponsor Halliday for reelection.

59. _____ 719

60. Entreprenuers in search of funding often submit glamorous proposals.

60. _____ 720

61. Our last mail campain did not pull very many orders.

61. _____ 720

62. Plagiarism is the only explanation for this amount of parralel wording.

62. _____ 720

63. It was presumptious of Vic to criticize the proposal.

63. _____ 720

64. The color of the stationary and the envelopes should be quite light.

64. _____ 719

65. We'll need to take out a second morgage to cover these expenses.

65. _____ 720

18 Compound Words

Directions: Underline every word or phrase that is misspelled or misused, and write the correct form in the answer column. If a sentence is correct, write *C* in the answer column. **References:** ¶¶801–812.

1. We need to get some feed-back from our sales reps in the South.

   1. _____ 803h

2. Ellen Berkowitz has served as secretary treasurer for two years.

   2. _____ 806 / 811

3. I prefer to have all my drafts typed triple spaced.

   3. _____ 812a

4. Simply place a checkmark next to each item you want to order.

   4. _____ 801a

5. Let's weed out the ones with real talent from the wannabes.

   5. _____ 804a

6. Sheila Grove, 37, has been named executive vice president of the Lombard-Rosetti Agency.

   6. _____ 808c

7. We need to hire more salesmen to handle this new product line.

   7. _____ 809a

8. When air conditioning an office, be sure to check the wiring.

   8. _____ 812a

9. Bev has a reputation for troubleshooting and problem solving.

   9. _____ 805a

10. Please follow-up with Bellows if he doesn't respond by Friday.

   10. _____ 802

Directions: Insert hyphens as necessary in each boldface group of words. Circle all hyphens you insert. If a sentence is correct as given, write *C* in the answer column. **References:** ¶¶813–847. Give special attention to ¶¶813–815.

11. We are hoping to get a **30 year** mortgage on a Victorian farmhouse that is more than **100 years old**.

   11. _____ 813 / 817a / 818a

12. This **medical insurance** policy does not cover **preexisting** conditions.

   12. _____ 835a / 831a

13. We build **state of the art turnkey** installations for public agencies.

   13. _____ 830a / 833d

14. The **pro and antiunion** forces are each running a **hard hitting** campaign.

   14. _____ 822a / 817a

15. I'd like you to recast the **five year** sales figures in your **long range** plan.

   15. _____ 816a / 818c

16. **Small business** owners are finding it hard to meet their **break even** point.

   16. _____ 829a / 824b

17. Frank is **well known** for his **no nonsense** approach to marketing.

   17. _____ 815a / 818b

18. Can we be sure these **cost benefit** projections are **up to date**?

   18. _____ 831a / 820a

19. Call us **toll free** on these **day and nighttime** phone numbers.

   19. _____ 832d / 824b

20. The operating instructions are **well illustrated** and are **self explanatory.**

   20. _____ 836a

21. Please be sure that all items on the form are properly **filled in**.

   21. _____ 826 / 831c

22. An **ad hoc** committee has been formed to make a **go/no go** decision.

   22. _____ 831d / 831a

23. Where can I find some **time tested** guidelines for **nonprofit** organizations?

   23. _____ 833a / 816a

24. Our **highest priority** goal is to boost our **bottom line** results by 12 percent.

   24. _____ 814

25. All tickets will be sold on a **first come, first served** basis.

   25. _____ 831d

26. Please get me **up to date** costs on **off the shelf** financial software.

   26. _____ 831a

27. You will be eligible for **social security** benefits in another six months.   27. _____ 818a
                                                                                              824a
28. The **newly formed** division will focus exclusively on **high tech** products.   28. _____ 814
29. Even if we suffer a **short term** loss, the **long term** prospects are excellent.   29. _____ 816a
30. Let's get a couple of bids on **recovering** the reception room furniture.   30. _____ 837
                                                                                              827b
31. There are no **hard and fast** rules for this type of **freewheeling** situation.   31. _____ 824d
                                                                                              833a
32. Our first hint of an **antitrust** suit came from a **high ranking** source.   32. _____ 822a
                                                                                              831e
33. The company has a **rinky dink** setup with a lot of **Mickey Mouse** procedures.   33. _____ 819a
                                                                                              820a
34. All contributions to Project Hope are **tax deductible**.   34. _____ 847f
                                                                                              822b
35. Our new **Web site** design is **better looking** than the old one.   35. _____ 816a
                                                                                              833a
36. Mr. Paley wants a **first class** ticket on a **nonstop** flight to Singapore.   36. _____ 832
37. There will be a **three to four month** delay until we get new **laptops**.   37. _____ 847e
                                                                                              828a
38. This **hit or miss** attitude toward quality is an **industrywide** problem.   38. _____ 820c
                                                                                              831b
39. Running a **mom and pop** kind of business can be quite **time consuming**.   39. _____ 821d
                                                                                              816a
40. Sandy has a **part time** job now but hopes to work **full time** this spring.   40. _____ 833a
                                                                                              824a
41. The latest **semiannual** report shows a **steadily increasing** demand for VCRs.   41. _____ 819b
                                                                                              816a
42. Please check the **Chicago Phoenix** plane schedules and the **round trip** fare.   42. _____ 817a
                                                                                              818a
43. Effective April 1, there will be a **13.5 percent** jump in **auto insurance** rates.   43. _____ 823a
44. These **high priced, steel belted** tires will last longer than your present tires.   44. _____ 821a
                                                                                              825b
45. Upon retirement I plan to follow a **less demanding, slower paced** schedule.   45. _____ 823b
                                                                                              831a
46. We expect to have some **out of town** visitors in **mid July**.   46. _____ 838
                                                                                              826
47. Our new contract with the company contains a **built in cost of living** clause.   47. _____ 831a

Directions: Rewrite the following sentences to correct all errors and remove sexist expressions. **References:** ¶¶801–847. For the rules on sexist expressions, see ¶¶809–810 and 840.

48. Businessmen need to follow-up with their sub-ordinates to avoid any break down in operations.

    _____

    _____
    809a
    802
    833a
    802

49. Ethel Kaplan, the well known authoress, will embark on a six-weeks' tour of the Mid-West.

    _____
    824b
    840a
    817a
    838

50. The chairman of every committee should spot check the on line records to ensure they are

    up-to-date. _____
    809d
    811
    847b
    831a

51. The woman surgeon who operated on my mother in law sees a 50 50 chance of a flare up in
    810
    839
    the pain. _____
    817c
    802
    803a

52. Send your congressman an E mail to protest the state wide campaign to build on government
    809d
    owned land. _____
    847d
    820c
    821a

19

Word Division

Directions: On each line below, there is one word that is *incorrectly* divided or that does *not* follow the preferred style of word division. Write the identifying letter for that word in the answer column. **References:** ¶¶901–922; a dictionary (optional).

1. **a.** prefer-/ ring	**b.** permit-/ ted	**c.** shun-/ ned	**d.** win-/ ner	1. _____	902 / 922
2. **a.** pre-/ arranged	**b.** recre-/ ation	**c.** re-/ act	**d.** re-/ ach	2. _____	901c / 914
3. **a.** rebel-/ ling	**b.** clip-/ ping	**c.** confer-/ ring	**d.** surpas-/ sing	3. _____	901c / 922
4. **a.** up-/ on	**b.** up-/ per	**c.** up-/ roar	**d.** up-/ date	4. _____	904
5. **a.** la-/ tent	**b.** par-/ ent	**c.** would-/ n't	**d.** war-/ rant	5. _____	906
6. **a.** recall-/ ing	**b.** impell-/ ing	**c.** misspell-/ ing	**d.** pull-/ ing	6. _____	922
7. **a.** a-/ broad	**b.** ab-/ duct	**c.** ab-/ sorb	**d.** ab-/ stract	7. _____	903a
8. **a.** re-/ cap	**b.** mad-/ cap	**c.** fools-/ cap	**d.** AS-/ CAP	8. _____	905
9. **a.** mas-/ terpiece	**b.** weather-/ proof	**c.** time-/ saving	**d.** share-/ holder	9. _____	907
10. **a.** para-/ legal	**b.** anti-/ septic	**c.** un-/ derneath	**d.** inter-/ office	10. _____	909
11. **a.** air-/ conditioned	**b.** weather-/ beaten	**c.** old-/ fashioned	**d.** govern-/ ment-owned	11. _____	908
12. **a.** in-/ terpret	**b.** in-/ ternal	**c.** super-/ fluous	**d.** ex-/ traordinary	12. _____	909
13. **a.** buzz-/ ing	**b.** swell-/ ing	**c.** barr-/ ing	**d.** cross-/ ing	13. _____	922
14. **a.** responsi-/ ble	**b.** prob-/ able	**c.** change-/ able	**d.** fea-/ sible	14. _____	910
15. **a.** bat-/ tle	**b.** diff-/ ered	**c.** pas-/ senger	**d.** mar-/ ried	15. _____	922
16. **a.** un-/ helpful	**b.** nonsmok-/ ing	**c.** retire-/ ment	**d.** prevail-/ ing	16. _____	911
17. **a.** pay-/ off	**b.** print-/ out	**c.** check-/ up	**d.** break-/ down	17. _____	904
18. **a.** continu-/ ation	**b.** patrio-/ tic	**c.** courte-/ ous	**d.** ingredi-/ ent	18. _____	914
19. **a.** help-/ fulness	**b.** meaning-/ ful	**c.** hopeless-/ ness	**d.** sportsman-/ ship	19. _____	911
20. **a.** break-/ up,	**b.** cave-/ in;	**c.** mark-/ down	**d.** mark-/ up	20. _____	904
21. **a.** man-/ agement	**b.** inter-/ national	**c.** follow-/ ing	**d.** pre-/ occupied	21. _____	912
22. **a.** para-/ lyze	**b.** log-/ ical	**c.** specu-/ late	**d.** ele-/ gant	22. _____	913
23. **a.** unluck-/ y,	**b.** trade-/ in;	**c.** stand-/ by?	**d.** line-/ up:	23. _____	903a / 901c
24. **a.** cIan-/ nish	**b.** regret-/ table	**c.** control-/ ler	**d.** spel-/ ling	24. _____	922 / 901c
25. **a.** be-/ lieve	**b.** soc-/ iety	**c.** vari-/ ety	**d.** pa-/ tience	25. _____	914
26. **a.** con-/ nect	**b.** cor-/ rect	**c.** coll-/ ect	**d.** cof-/ fee	26. _____	922
27. **a.** micro-/ chip	**b.** eye-/ witness	**c.** paper-/ work	**d.** moneylend-/ ers	27. _____	907
28. **a.** improve-/ ment	**b.** bor-/ rowing	**c.** hyper-/ active	**d.** under-/ developed	28. _____	912
29. **a.** neg-/ ative	**b.** rele-/ vant	**c.** moni-/ tor	**d.** salu-/ tation	29. _____	913
30. **a.** im-/ mobile	**b.** hum-/ ming	**c.** skim-/ med	**d.** ham-/ mer	30. _____	902 / 922

Directions: Rewrite each word in the answer column to indicate the preferred word division at the end of a line. If a word cannot be divided, put a dash in the answer column. **References:** ¶¶901–922; a dictionary (optional).

#	Word	Answer	Ref	#	Word	Answer	Ref
31.	similar	_____	913	41.	connection	_____	912
32.	thoughtfulness	_____	911	42.	muffled	_____	922c
33.	repayable	_____	910	43.	markup	_____	904
34.	expressed	_____	901c 914	44.	$429,600	_____	915
35.	straightforward	_____	907	45.	self-conscious	_____	908
36.	about	_____	903a	46.	continuation	_____	914
37.	announce	_____	922c 903a	47.	strength	_____	902
38.	piano	_____	914 903a	48.	shouldn't	_____	906
39.	amusement	_____	910	49.	addressed	_____	901c 922c
40.	circumstances	_____	909	50.	UNICEF	_____	905

Directions: In the following entries a diagonal rule is used to suggest where one typed line ends and another begins. If the line ending does not reflect preferred style, draw a new diagonal line to indicate a better point of word division. (If there is more than one way to improve the word division, draw the new diagonal line as close as possible to the old one.) If the line ending is acceptable as given, write OK in the answer column. **References:** ¶¶915–920.

51. The reunion luncheon has been scheduled for June/ 4, 2007, at the Alumni
Club . . .   51. _____ 920a

52. We had hoped to raise $50,-/ 000 in this year's campaign for homeless shelters . . .   52. _____ 915

53. On the basis of the lab reports, Dr./ Cortines recommends that . . .   53. _____ 919

54. Our main distribution center is only 14/ miles from . . .   54. _____ 919

55. This year's luncheon speaker is Attorney/ General Jane Minetta . . .   55. _____ 920g

56. You will have to ask Thomas Gilmartin/ Jr., who drafted the proposal . . .   56. _____ 919

57. The Fulton Literary Prize was awarded to Ms. Celia/ R. Gomez . . .   57. _____ 920d

58. The annotated bibliography on page/ 236 offers . . .   58. _____ 919

59. We have leased new offices at 680 Pennington/ Boulevard . . .   59. _____ 920b

60. Let's plan to get together in my office on May/ 2 at 3 o'clock . . .   60. _____ 919

61. You can send it to my summer home in Cohasset,/ Massachusetts 02025 . . .   61. _____ 920c

62. Let's talk with Bart Elliott/ —he's the general manager of . . .   62. _____ 920k

63. I urge you to read Chapter/ 7 for its trenchant analysis of . . .   63. _____ 919

64. Total annual sales (domestic and foreign) now exceed $12,000,-/ 000,000 . . .   64. _____ 915

65. The meeting should end by 10/ p.m. at the latest . . .   65. _____ 919

66. . . . will have three main objectives: (1)/ to determine how . . .   66. _____ 920j

67. Gateway Industries has announced the promotion of Jay Tracy/ II to . . .   67. _____ 919

68.   We are pleased to announce that Janice Krauss will be join-/   68. _____ 917

69. ing our staff as a senior account executive. She has previous-/   69. _____ 904

70. ly served as a copywriter for several top-rated agencies, work-/
ing with such clients as . . .   70. _____ 916

20 Editing Survey C

Directions: Supply missing punctuation and strike out or correct any inappropriate punctuation in the following material. Change the spelling as necessary. Circle all changes you make. **References:** Sections 6–9.

Since the 1990's users of personal computers have been quiet likely to encounter **1**
computer viruses that have been concocted by mischievious hackers or malicious weirdoes to erase **2**
computer data and software programs. A computer virus is actually a small program in itself **3**
that manages to infiltrate other programs, data files, and operating systems. It typically spre- **4**
ads as "infected" e-mail messages, documents, and programs are forwarded to different PC's. **5**
One can readily conjure up a series of hair raising scenarioes for disaster, but it's difficult **6**
to concieve the motivation of the people who master-mind the creation of these viruses. **7**

The problem was dramatically high-lighted by the world-wide appearance of a virus named **8**
Michelangelo. The virus was named for the fifteenth century Italian artist, because on March 6, 1992 **9**
(the occasion of Michelangelo's 517th birthday), the virus, which had been quietly spreading **10**
for a while, was designed to attack IBM computers as well as IBM compatible equipment. **11**
According to a news' article that appeared on that day in *The New York Times*, this virus was **12**
first detected in Germany in 1991. Because of the advance warning, most users succeded in **13**
elimanating the virus before it could effect their programs. Indeed, manufacturers of anti-viral **14**
programs profited handsomely from the demand for devices that could protect equipment **15**
otherwise susceptible to serious damage from the virus. **16**

In August 2003 three powerful viruses spread over hundreds of thousands of computers. **17**
The MSBlaster virus attacked 120,000 computers in one 24 hour period alone. This virus searched **18**
the Internet for vulnerable computers, forcing many to shut down every time they reconnected to **19**
the Internet. **20**

There are several ways to fight computer viruses—each with it's own pro's and con's— **21**
but many computer companys did not start to make use of their know how until customers **22**
began to demand this kind of security. There is now a concencus among knowledgable people **23**
in the field, who say that personal computers must be redesigned to provide the neccessary **24**
protection. **25**

Lance J. Hoffman, a computer expert sited in the *Times* article, put the whole issue in **26**
clear prospective: "It's just like automobiles. When people got tired of seeing people thrown **27**
out on the highway after accidents, they began adding seat belts. We need the equivalent of **28**
seat belts built into our computers." **29**

Directions: Supply missing punctuation and strike out or correct any inappropriate punctuation in the following material. Change the spelling as necessary. Circle all changes you make. **References:** Sections 6–9.

If you often have material that needs to be copied—indeed, if you are running a home based   **1**

business—you are familar with the frustration of continuously going out to the copy shop or waiting   **2**

in line at the liberry. In that case, you're definately going to welcome the news about the increased   **3**

affordability of compact photocopiers designed specifically for home use. These home copiers   **4**

have become so popular that they now sell well over 500,000 units a year in this country.   **5**

Today's easy to use models can come in handy for a variety of purposes. You can convenient-   **6**

ly reproduce legal documents, tax records, cancelled checks, notices, and reciepts—and even your   **7**

childrens' report cards. The equipment is so user friendly that youngsters can copy their own   **8**

homework and drawings.   **9**

What has made these compact copiers feasable is a technology that eliminates the need for   **10**

a service technician to replace the toner (a powder that melts to form images) and the photo-   **11**

conducting element (typically a drum that transfers the toner onto the copy paper). These   **12**

elements can now be supplied in no muss, no fuss cartridges. As a result, most small copiers   **13**

will yeild high quality reproductions on almost any type of paper.   **14**

You will find that prices for these desktop copiers are relatively low when they are compar-   **15**

ed with the prices for typical office equipment. The basic machine carries a list price of   **16**

$150 to $300, but you can often get as much as a 60-percent discount. The replacable toner   **17**

cartridges typically cost between $10 and $120; they usually make between 1000 and 3500   **18**

copies, and some make as many as 11,500. Replaceable drums cost between $120 and $140,   **19**

and cartridges containing both the toner and the drum cost between $90 and $125. If you   **20**

consider just the cost of the paper and the cartridges, the average cost for each copy can range   **21**

from 3 to 14 cents. If you also figure in some tiny fraction of what it cost to purchase the copier   **22**

itself, the cost for each copy is much higher. In other words, the cost of making copies at home   **23**

is not exactly a bargain.   **24**

Since capabilitys vary, you should carefully compare the pro's and con's of the different   **25**

machines and pick the one that best fits your needs and your wallet. For example, some copiers   **26**

can make legal size copies; others can make only the standard 8½ by 11 inch copies. Some will   **27**

make enlargements and reductions, some will accept computer print-outs, and some will   **28**

copy pages strait from bound books. You should also consider differences in the copiers' speed   **29**

of operation. Some can produce as many as 10 or 11 copies a minute; others produce only 3 or   **30**

4 copies a minute. In any case, it can take 10 to 30 seconds for the first copy to appear.   **31**

Before you procede to buy a compact copier, you ought to way the investment in equipment   **32**

and supplies against the cost of making copies commercially. In most large cities single copy   **33**

rates can range from 5 to 10 cents. If you will not be making a large number of copies at one time,   **34**

consider a budget priced machine with a minimum of controls and special features.   **35**

21 Subjects and Verbs

Directions: Select the correct form in parentheses, and write your answer in the column at the right. **References:** ¶¶1001–1048.

1. Every investor and saver (has, have) become more cautious recently.
2. Neither the directors nor the top executives (wants, want) to relocate.
3. Only one of the photocopiers (is, are) working properly.
4. One of the causes for the breakdowns (is, are) poor maintenance.
5. (Has, Have) any of your customers complained about deliveries?
6. The criteria for paying bonuses (has, have) to be rethought.
7. *Changing Times* (is, are) offering subscribers a special renewal rate.
8. Over three-quarters of the draft (has, have) to be rewritten.
9. There (has, have) been no news from Frank in two months.
10. Those who (did, done) the customer survey deserve much praise.
11. It is critical that this memo (is, be) distributed this afternoon.
12. More than one client (has, have) asked me whether Chris is leaving.
13. Neither management nor the union (likes, like) the settlement.
14. Mr. Hall, along with his two partners, (is, are) going to Paris today.
15. (Has, Have) their board voted yet on the reorganization plan?
16. The number of job openings (has, have) increased this month.
17. Many of our salespeople have (rose, risen) quickly to higher-level jobs.
18. Paul said that he (will, would) debug the program over the weekend.
19. Kate is one of those people who (writes, write) well without effort.
20. None of the applicants (impress, impresses) either of us very much.
21. I wish I (was, were) going to be considered for Larry's job.
22. Many on the sales staff (wants, want) to attend the seminar.
23. Either of the editors (is, are) willing to take on your manuscript.
24. Brooks Brothers (is, are) having its annual sale next week.
25. Twenty dollars (doesn't, don't) buy much these days.
26. If I had heard, I would (tell, have told) you the news.
27. One of the products we distribute (is, are) coffee grinders.
28. A number of my customers (has, have) asked for bigger discounts.
29. Attached (is, are) three layouts for you to evaluate and choose from.
30. Every one of us (hopes, hope) you will have a speedy recovery.

#	Answer	Reference
1.	_____	1002c / 1009b
2.	_____	1004
3.	_____	1006a / 1008a
4.	_____	1006a / 1008a
5.	_____	1013a
6.	_____	1018a
7.	_____	1022
8.	_____	1025a
9.	_____	1014 / 1028a
10.	_____	1032b
11.	_____	1038a
12.	_____	1013a
13.	_____	1003
14.	_____	1007
15.	_____	1019a
16.	_____	1023
17.	_____	1033
18.	_____	1047
19.	_____	1008b
20.	_____	1013b
21.	_____	1039a
22.	_____	1012
23.	_____	1009a
24.	_____	1020
25.	_____	1024
26.	_____	1040
27.	_____	1008a / 1029a
28.	_____	1023
29.	_____	1027a
30.	_____	1010

Name _____ Date _____ Class _____ 43

Directions: Underline all errors in the following sentences, and write the correct forms in the answer column. If a sentence is correct, write *C* in the answer column. **References:** ¶¶1001–1048.

31. Many a trainer and instructor have been helped by your techniques. 31. _____ 1002c / 1009b
32. Not only the workers but also the management favors a four-day week. 32. _____ 1005
33. Our arrangements with the Dodd Service Agency has worked out quite well. 33. _____ 1006a
34. Your survey, along with Fox's study, prove that the supplier was at fault. 34. _____ 1007 / 1008a
35. One of the factors we consider in choosing suppliers are fast service. 35. _____ 1029a
36. Olive is the only one of our employees who are consistently on time. 36. _____ 1008c / 1002c
37. Every art director and designer on staff wants to work on the Athens account. 37. _____ 1009b
38. Few of the people I talked with actually believes the merger will occur. 38. _____ 1012
39. More than six people have turned down the chance to work for Alix. 39. _____ 1013a
40. Although most of our stock is selling well, some of the goods isn't moving. 40. _____ 1013a / 1015
41. A series of management seminars have been planned for the fall. 41. _____ 1016
42. With the right teacher, economics is a fascinating subject. 42. _____ 1017 / 1023
43. The number of new competitors has rose at an alarming rate. 43. _____ 1033
44. That the HMO plan offers many advantages are not to be denied. 44. _____ 1026a
45. Yet only a small percentage of our employees has chosen the HMO plan. 45. _____ 1025a
46. Here is a descriptive brochure and a sample copy of the book. 46. _____ 1028a
47. The photocopying equipment on the seventh floor has broke down again. 47. _____ 1033
48. It is urgent that Frank responds quickly to the job offer. 48. _____ 1038b
49. I wish it was the end and not the start of the holiday rush. 49. _____ 1039a
50. It is the sales reps who want the pricing schedule adjusted. 50. _____ 1029a

Directions: Rewrite the following sentences to correct all errors and remove awkward expressions. **References:** ¶¶1005, 1007, 1010, 1018, 1019, 1032, 1033, 1037, 1046, and 1048.

51. Everyone of us want to thank you for all that you done. _____ 1010 / 1032 / 1033a
_____

52. I have always thought and still do that our problems begun when the Troy plant was sold by us.
_____ 1048 / 1032 / 1037b
_____

53. The whole staff, including John and me, think the books should be audited by you at once.
_____ 1019a / 1007 / 1037b
_____

54. The board is not able to agree on whether to immediately raise prices. _____ 1019b / 1046
_____

55. The criteria for acceptable performance has been established, but neither the employees nor the manager understands them._____ 1018a / 1005
_____

22 Pronouns and Other Grammar Problems

Directions: Select the correct form in parentheses, and write your answer in the column at the right. **References:** ¶¶1049–1088.

1. The company has given (its, their) managers new productivity goals.
2. A number of you have not yet signed (their, your) commission contracts.
3. Bob can make the presentation a lot more effectively than (I, me).
4. (Who, Whom) should we invite as the keynote speaker?
5. This year's convention displays look (real, really) handsome.
6. Given the two alternatives, I think you chose the (best, better) plan.
7. They have asked for no discount (or, nor) any other special terms.
8. These price increases are retroactive (to, from) October 15.
9. Neither Bert nor Jerry can lend us (his, their) boat for the weekend.
10. It was Jan and (me, I) who made all the arrangements for the banquet.
11. Every company has (its, it's) own policy on promotions and transfers.
12. This is the kind of case that (us, we) lawyers find truly challenging.
13. We want to know (who, whom) you think will be appointed.
14. We feel very (bad, badly) about your decision to move out of the area.
15. I have decided that I do not want (any, no) part of the money.
16. The monitor you shipped us does not correspond (to, with) the one described in your brochure.
17. Please let that be a private matter between you and (me, I).
18. Jack is a person (who's, whose) reputation for fairness is well known.
19. This trip to Scandinavia will be a dream come true for my family and (me, myself).
20. This is a problem every adult faces with (their, his or her) parents.

1.	1049a
2.	1053d
3.	1057
4.	1061d
5.	1065
6.	1071g
7.	1076c
8.	1077
9.	1049c
10.	1054b
11.	1056e
12.	1058
13.	1061c
14.	1067
15.	1076a
16.	1077
17.	1055b
18.	1063
19.	1060d
20.	1050 / 1052a

Directions: Underline all errors in the following sentences, and write the correct forms in the answer column. If a sentence is correct, write *C* in the answer column. **References:** ¶¶1049–1088.

21. Either Lois or Pam can lend you their procedures manual.
22. If anyone has already paid the fee, he or she should ask for a refund.
23. Ball's use of company funds looks highly questionable to we auditors.
24. I have no questions nor concerns about the terms of the contract.
25. We can fill your orders just as quickly and as cheaply as them.

21.	1049c
22.	1053a
23.	1058
24.	1076c
25.	1057

Name _____ Date _____ Class _____

26. Rita considered you and I to be sisters or at least first cousins.   **26.** _____   1064a

27. It is you who has to make the first move toward reconciliation.   **27.** _____   1049a

28. No one will represent the firm at the trade fair except you and I.   **28.** _____   1055b

29. George Fry and myself hosted the party for the Kennellys.   **29.** _____   1060d

30. Please deliver these tapes to whomever is in charge of the studio.   **30.** _____   1061c

31. It's clear that they're marketing strategy is more effective than ours.   **31.** _____   1056e

32. Whom do you think will apply for Larry Kenilworth's job in Finance?   **32.** _____   1061c

33. The commission will issue their long-awaited ruling on Monday.   **33.** _____   1049a

Directions: Rewrite the following sentences to correct all errors, fix awkward or ungrammatical constructions, and remove sexist expressions. **References:** ¶¶1049–1088. For the rules on sexist expressions, see ¶¶1050–¶1053.

34. Neither the sales representatives nor the sales manager has submitted his expense report.

_____

_____   1049c

35. Everyone in Marketing should submit his catalog copy no later than July 20. _____

_____   1053a

36. Rhode Island is smaller than any state in the Union. _____

_____   1071h

37. To ensure a full refund, the original sales slip should be sent along with the merchandise.

_____

_____   1082b

38. If a customer asks for Model B-1101, tell him that we are out of stock. _____

_____   1050

_____   1052b

39. Randy only plans to take two courses next summer. _____

_____   1072

40. We got off the plane at about 11:45 p.m. _____

_____   1078

41. Your performance not only moved the audience but also the other members of the cast. _____

_____   1081b

42. In auditing your account, two discrepancies were noted by my assistant. _____

_____   1082c

43. This year's profit goals are much higher than last year. _____

_____   1071i

44. We don't get many inquiries, or many requests for, these oil lamps. _____

_____   1079

23 Usage

Directions: Select the correct form in parentheses, and write your answer in the column at the right. **References:** Section 11. The individual entries are listed alphabetically. If you have difficulty in finding an entry, consult the list at the start of Section 11 (on pages 308–310 of *The Gregg Reference Manual*).

1. (A, An) M.B.A. degree would surely bring you better job offers.

1. _____

2. The loss of two programmers will greatly (affect, effect) our output.

2. _____

3. Mary Lee is (already, all ready) to take on her new assignment.

3. _____

4. We'll be glad to help in (anyway, any way) that we can.

4. _____

5. A large (amount, number) of people visited our convention exhibit.

5. _____

6. Simply ignore the problem for (awhile, a while) and see what happens.

6. _____

7. The reason we lost the deal is (because, that) our offer was topped.

7. _____

8. If Frank (don't, doesn't) like the new procedure, he should say why.

8. _____

9. Does anyone (beside, besides) Bo know our CEO very well?

9. _____

10. Our sales have dropped (due to, because of) new competition.

10. _____

11. I urged Sam to delve (farther, further) into the reasons for heavy returns.

11. _____

12. We've had (fewer, less) complaints since the product was redesigned.

12. _____

13. (First, Firstly), you need to streamline your approval procedures.

13. _____

14. You'll have to take another (tack, tact) if you want to change Ed's mind.

14. _____

15. I doubt (if, whether) we'll be able to make the party on the 15th.

15. _____

16. From what Sue said, I (implied, inferred) that she won't be back.

16. _____

17. Fred has been (laying, lying) down on the job lately.

17. _____

18. There (maybe, may be) some truth to the story after all.

18. _____

19. More (important, importantly), this model carries a lower price tag.

19. _____

20. Anyone could (of, have) seen through that ruse.

20. _____

21. Bond prices have been (raising, rising) all this quarter.

21. _____

22. You can (set, sit) the easel in my office while I'm gone.

22. _____

23. I will call Mary myself (so, so that) we can get to the bottom of this.

23. _____

24. Glen saw her at Lake Tahoe (sometime, some time) ago.

24. _____

25. We (sure, surely) appreciate all you have done for us.

25. _____

26. Most of our customers prefer (this, these) kind of printer.

26. _____

27. If you (would have, had) told me your arrival time, I would have met you at the airport.

27. _____

28. We are all (anxious, eager) to get the scoop on our merger with Cali Co.

28. _____

29. I don't know (as, whether) I can reveal that information.

29. _____

30. I am writing (in regard to, in regards to) your order of April 12.

30. _____

Name _____ Date _____ Class _____

47

Directions: If the boldface word or phrase is correct, write *C* in the answer column. If the word or phrase is incorrect, supply the correct form. **References:** Section 11.

31. My notes for the minutes of the meeting were **accidently** thrown out.　31. _____

32. It has been taking us **all together** too long to get new products out in the marketplace.　32. _____

33. Mrs. Penney's estate will be equally split **between** her six children.　33. _____

34. Please keep me **appraised** of any falloff in our international sales.　34. _____

35. We all feel very **badly** about the way Ted has treated you.　35. _____

36. Whatever information passes between you and **me** is confidential.　36. _____

37. In **less** than five years our firm has achieved a statewide reputation.　37. _____

38. Our new warehouse is **further** out from the downtown district.　38. _____

39. I **graduated** from Emory University with a B.S. in economics.　39. _____

40. It looks **like** you may have a winner on your hands after all.　40. _____

41. I feel my supervisor treats me **different** from the others on her staff.　41. _____

42. What **kind of an** outcome do you want this letter to produce?　42. _____

43. Because of her asthma Jean needs to move to a **healthier** climate.　43. _____

44. Please come **into** see me when you are next in town.　44. _____

45. The new floor plan was **laying** on her desk where anyone could see it.　45. _____

46. Will you please **leave** me see the summary of your report?　46. _____

47. I would like you to check **upon** our new customer service procedures.　47. _____

48. The weather this winter has been **real** mild.　48. _____

49. I received your letter and will answer **same** next week.　49. _____

50. We try to **service** our customers efficiently and courteously.　50. _____

51. Be **sure and** stop by when you next get to Nashville.　51. _____

52. Our market share is much greater **then** it was three years ago.　52. _____

53. Both sides in the dispute are slowly moving **towards** a compromise.　53. _____

54. Our partnership has come a long **ways** since we started in 1999.　54. _____

55. This new product line will put us **indirect** competition with Bascom.　55. _____

56. I think **this here** layout works better than anything else I've seen.　56. _____

57. Stan hopes that **a** M.B.A. degree will get him a better-paying job.　57. _____

58. Since you made the service call, everything has worked **alright.**　58. _____

59. Please **bring** the contracts to Mr. Hellman when you go to visit him.　59. _____

60. I wish we knew who **done** the original construction.　60. _____

61. Will they be able to **learn** me how to improve my English?　61. _____

62. Your procedure is different **than** the one I learned in school.　62. _____

63. The two of us need to sound out **one another's** ideas before we go to the conference.　63. _____

64. These power outages are becoming an **everyday** affair.　64. _____

65. **Everyone** of these customer complaints needs to be fully investigated.　65. _____

24 Usage (Continued)

Directions: If the boldface word or phrase is correct as given, write *C* in the answer column. If the word or phrase is incorrect, supply the correct form in the answer column. **References:** Section 11. The individual entries are listed alphabetically. If you have difficulty in finding an entry, consult the full listing of entries at the start of Section 11 (on pages 308–310 of *The Gregg Reference Manual*).

1. What strategies are likely to have a significant **affect** on our output?   1. _____

2. We plan to mail this questionnaire to people **age** 55 and up.   2. _____

3. We were **almost** relieved to hear of your son's recovery from surgery.   3. _____

4. My husband is not doing too **bad** since he took early retirement.   4. _____

5. I'll make a point of seating you **besides** the speaker.   5. _____

6. The statements and the checks should be **altogether** in the red file folder.   6. _____

7. I don't doubt **but what** you'll get the fellowship you applied for.   7. _____

8. I doubt **if** we can still make the target date for our fall ad campaign.   8. _____

9. Any success I've achieved has been largely **due to** the staff support I got.   9. _____

10. We are willing to consider **always** of reducing our costs.   10. _____

11. Len, Gary, and I will undertake identical research studies and then share the data with **each other**.   11. _____

12. **Everyone** has to work at the convention booth except you and me.   12. _____

13. Let's not sell the condo for **awhile** in case prices start to go up again.   13. _____

14. The fabric comes in red, blue, and purple, but I prefer the **former.**   14. _____

15. I bought a van with only 12,000 miles on it **off** a tennis partner of mine.   15. _____

16. The noise was so loud that we **couldn't hardly** hear ourselves.   16. _____

17. In telling me about the reorganization, Frank **inferred** that he would be promoted to assistant vice president.   17. _____

18. **Incidently,** what more have you heard about the Kossoff investigation?   18. _____

19. Andy seemed **in different** when I told him my plans.   19. _____

20. We can make no exceptions to this policy, **irregardless** of the situation.   20. _____

21. You **can** take Monday off as long as you make up the time.   21. _____

22. **Most all** of the backlog of orders has now been cleaned up.   22. _____

23. I know of **no body** on the staff with those qualifications.   23. _____

24. Ben should **of** told us he was planning to sell his interest in the firm.   24. _____

25. It's time for us to move **onto** a new topic for discussion.   25. _____

26. We have a real **dilemma** when it comes to dealing with the cost of health insurance.   26. _____

27. I was doing 78 miles **per** hour when the police pulled me over.   27. _____

Name _____   Date _____   Class _____   49

28. I will try **and** get you price quotes from several suppliers by Friday.   28. _____

29. **Who ever** heard of a top-quality DVD recorder for under $500?   29. _____

30. It may be better, **than,** to put our decision off until next month.   30. _____

Directions: Rewrite the following sentences to correct all errors in usage. **References:** Section 11.

31. The reason for our inventory problems is because a large percent of our product line is outmoded.

_____

_____

32. We are cutting costs travelwise, per your mandate. _____

_____

33. I could not help from smiling at that kind of a snappy comeback. _____

_____

34. The reviews for both albums were equally as good, but we couldn't find copies of either, however.

_____

_____

35. The amount of compliments we received on our new showroom was kind of impressive.

_____

36. Everyone of us enthused over the way the play ended up. _____

_____

37. I cannot help but remember my one encounter with former President Carter. _____

_____

38. Television is the one media that we don't scarcely use for our ad campaigns. _____

_____

39. Being that we both like these kind of mineral water, why don't we split a case among us?

_____

40. The latest train leaves the main terminal at about 11:30 p.m. _____

_____

41. Incidently, yesterday Joe served us an excellent breakfast of melon, cereal, bacon and eggs.

_____

_____

42. Less men these days are buying items such as hats and ties, etc. _____

_____

43. Please lie the sketch down carefully so it doesn't smudge. _____

_____

44. Like I warned you before, your failure to pay these bills will seriously effect your credit rating.

_____

45. Come and see me, Ed, when you have sometime to review my investment portfolio._____

_____

25 Editing Survey D

Directions: Edit the following material for errors in grammar and usage. Circle any changes you make. **References:** Sections 10–11.

The New York Times report regularly on new developments in computer technology. According	1
to a recent column by Peter H. Lewis, "As a drawing or painting tool, the computer mouse is only	2
slightly less effective than a potato." The limitations of the mouse has created special problems for	3
a large amount of people who's goal are to draw, paint, or trace images by means of a personal	4
computer.	5
A solution to the dilemma has been around for awhile in the form of graphics tablets that make	6
use of a cordless electronic stylus. This stylus is a kind of a pen that is pressure-sensitive. As a result,	7
the more pressure you apply, the thicker the line you create. In most cases, when you use this	8
stylus, the image shows up on the screen but not on the graphics tablet, however. For people who	9
are use to working on paper, there are electronic pens (and pencils) that write simultaneously	10
with real ink (or lead) and with electrons. In that way you can create images on paper and on the	11
screen at the same time.	12
Now comes an innovation that takes this technology farther. Who could of imagined an	13
electronic pen *with an eraser?* Well, its happened. Like the pen itself, the eraser is pressure-	14
sensitive. Thus the more harder you bear down on the tablet with the eraser, the more thorough	15
the erasing affect will be on the electronic image.	16
More importantly, you don't have to be an artist to appreciate the merits of an electronic pen	17
with an electronic eraser. The pen not only works with graphics programs but also with word	18
processing programs and other types of applications. More than one expert have noted that the pen	19
is actually more effective then a mouse in moving a cursor around on the screen, plus it can be used	20
to initiate the commands needed to delete words, paragraphs, cells, and other items on the screen.	21
What's more, by using this type electronic pen, your likely to develop less injuries, such as	22
mouse elbow (a repetitive strain injury very much like tennis elbow). The worse that can happen	23
when you use an electronic pen for a long period of time is an every day case of writer's cramp.	24
May be that's why alot of people are real anxious to get they're hands on this new technological	25
marvel.	26
Personal digital assistants (PDAs) and tablet PCs allow you to write text with the pen. The	27
software interprets the handwritten letters and converts them into typed characters on the screen.	28

Directions: Edit the following material for errors in grammar and usage. Circle any changes you make. **References:** Sections 1–11.

If you are buying your first personal computer, there is a number of devices you also need to **1**
buy. One purchase that requires real careful thought are printers. When considering which type **2**
printer to buy, one key criterion should be kept in mind: Do you want to print in color? Or are **3**
you content with black-and white results? **4**

If you work mainly with black-and-white text pages and high quality has to be insured, con- **5**
sider laser printers. This kind of a printer provides not only sharp, clear text but also turns **6**
out pages quickly and quietly. Laser printers use to cost thousands of dollars but now cost no **7**
more then $200 to $400. **8**

If the use of color is important in the work you do, consider buying a ink-jet printer. **9**
Good ink-jets are typically priced between $150–$400, but some can be found for as little as **10**
$50. Color laser printers are also available, but they are much too expensive (about $1000) for **11**
most home users. When you consider that (1) ink-jets provide excellent color printing, (2) in **12**
some cases they produce black-and-white pages as good as what you'd get from laser printers, **13**
and (3) they cost about the same as laser printers, you'd be tempted to conclude that ink-jets **14**
are the only smart choice. Yet there are other factors you need to take into account. **15**

1. *Speed. Consumer Reports* state that the laser printers its staff recently tested pro- **16**
   duce 9 to 15 black-and-white pages a minute. Whereas the ink-jets with **17**
   the best-looking black-and-white pages turn out between 2.5 and 9.5 pages a **18**
   minute. Good color printing takes much longer—2 to 18 minutes per page. **19**

2. *Quality.* Laser printers excel in producing black-and-white text at high speed, **20**
   but do less well with black-and-white graphics and photos. Ink-jets excel in **21**
   color work. **22**

3. *What About Cost?* The cost of a black-and-white page produced by an ink-jet **23**
   can range from 3 to 9 cents, compared to a cost of 2 to 4 cents for a simi- **24**
   lar page produced by a laser printer. Color printing is quite expensive: 8 **25**
   to 32 cents for color graphics and as much as $1.10 for color photos. **26**

At one time, when a computer user wanted to buy a printer for their home office and a major **27**
consideration were costs, the only real choice would of been a dot matrix printer. However, with the **28**
significant advances in technology, buying dot matrix printers no longer make sense. A large per- **29**
cent of these users now recognizes that laser and ink-jet printers provide superior performance on a **30**
cost-effective basis. Because of heavy competition the prices of printers have not rose lately. In **31**
fact, the prices of many models have fell this year, and next year's prices are expected to be lower **32**
than this year. Moreover, a new generation of printers are now being developed. With this **33**
continuing advance in technology comes new opportunities for high-quality printers at lower **34**
cost. **35**

26

Letters

Directions: For each of the following sentences choose the phrase that best completes the meaning of the sentence. Then in the answer column record the identifying letter for the phrase you selected. **References:** ¶¶1301–1341.

1. In what letter style do the date line, the complimentary closing, and the writer's identification start at center and all other lines start at the left margin: **(a)** the block style; **(b)** the simplified styles; **(c)** the modified-block style—standard format?

   1. _____ 1302a

2. What are the dimensions of *letter (standard)* stationery: **(a)** 8" × 11"; **(b)** 8½" × 11; **(c)** 8½" × 11½"?

   2. _____ 1303

3. To create a top margin of 2 inches, **(a)** space down 12 times from the top of the sheet; **(b)** space down 9 times; **(c)** space down 6 times from the default top margin of 1 inch.

   3. _____ 1304a

4. If you are using *letter (standard)* stationery and want to use a text line that is shorter than the standard, you can increase the default side margins up to **(a)** 1.5 inches; **(b)** 1.75 inches; **(c)** 2 inches.

   4. _____ 1305b

5. If you are writing to someone who rents a mailbox from a private company, place the private mailbox number **(a)** on the line above the name of the person; **(b)** on the line above the street address; **(c)** on the same line preceding the street address.

   5. _____ 1338d

6. *Standard* punctuation calls for **(a)** a comma or period at the end of each displayed line; **(b)** only a colon after the salutation and a comma after the complimentary closing; **(c)** no punctuation after any displayed line.

   6. _____ 1308a

7. Where should a personal or confidential notation be typed: **(a)** on the second line below the date, beginning at center; **(b)** on the second line below the date, beginning at the left margin; **(c)** on the second line below the date, ending at the right margin?

   7. _____ 1314

8. If there are no special notations following the date, then on what line below the date should the inside address begin: **(a)** on the fourth line; **(b)** on the fifth line; **(c)** on the sixth line?

   8. _____ 1318a

9. When a person's name ends with *Jr.*, **(a)** insert a comma before *Jr.*; **(b)** do not insert a comma before *Jr.*; **(c)** do not insert a comma before *Jr.* unless you know that is the person's preference.

   9. _____ 1324a

10. If an apartment number or a room number appears in an inside address, it should be typed **(a)** after the street address or on the line above; **(b)** after the street address or on the line below; **(c)** in the lower left corner of the envelope.

    10. _____ 1316b 1317b

11. You must always show the state name in an inside address as a two-letter abbreviation—**(a)** true; **(b)** false.

    11. _____ 1341a

12. Which of the following date line styles is *not* acceptable: **(a)** August 12, 2008; **(b)** 12 August 2008; **(c)** 8/12/08?

    12. _____ 1313a

13. When a company name ends with *Inc.*, **(a)** insert a comma before *Inc.*; **(b)** do not insert a comma before *Inc.*; **(c)** do not insert a comma before *Inc.*, unless you know that it is the company's preference.

    13. _____ 1328 1329b

Directions: Each of the items at the left represents an element in a business letter. If the item is correctly styled, write *C* in the answer column. If not, rewrite the item to make it correct. Assume the use of a **modified-block style—standard format** (¶1302a), **standard punctuation** (¶1308a), and **single spacing**. References: ¶¶1301–1341, plus ¶462 and ¶517a.

14. Jan. 29, 2007	**14.** _____	1313a
15. Confidential	**15.** _____	1314

Treat items 16–31 as they should appear in an **inside address**.

16. Ralph G. Ferrara, Jr. *(agrees with signature)*	**16.** _____	1322a 1324a
17. Kathleen A. Koch *(title preference unknown)*	**17.** _____	1322b
18. N. J. Harper	**18.** _____	1322c
19. Mr. & Mrs. Lloyd Welsh	**19.** _____	1323a
20. Doctor Nancy Fordyce	**20.** _____	517a 1322a
21. Mr. Royce Mead Esq.	**21.** _____	1324b
22. Dr. Sally Eng, M.D.	**22.** _____	1324c
23. Ms. Jan Corey, Director of Research and development	**23.** _____	1325
24. Marketing Department, Beta Aerospace Corporation	**24.** _____	1327
25. Capp & Rollins Co., Inc. *(no letterhead available)*	**25.** _____	1329
26. 764 Haskell St. N.E.	**26.** _____	1335a 1337
27. No. 163, 9th Avenue	**27.** _____	1332 1333a
28. #1 West Eleventh Street	**28.** _____	1332 1333b
29. 1,616 S. Fuller Blvd.	**29.** _____	462 1334 1337
30. Ft. Lauderdale, FL, 33315	**30.** _____	1340c 1339
31. Pittsburgh P.A. 15234	**31.** _____	1339 1341a
32. Dear Jane Reddy *(title preference unknown)*	**32.** _____	1339a
33. Dear Prof. Simcoe,	**33.** _____	1338d 1338b
34. Gentlemen:	**34.** _____	1340a
35. Australia	**35.** _____	1336a

54

27 Letters, Memos, and E-Mail

Directions: Choose the phrase that best completes the meaning of each of the following sentences. Then in the answer column record the identifying letter for the phrase you selected. Assume the use of a **modified-block style–standard format** (¶1302a), **standard punctuation** (¶1308a), and **single spacing. References:** ¶¶1352–1389.

1. A subject line, if used, should be typed **(a)** on the third line below the inside address; **(b)** on the third line below the salutation; **(c)** on the second line below the salutation.   1. ____1343a____

2. Begin the message of the letter **(a)** on the third line below the salutation (or subject line) at the left margin; **(b)** on the second line below the salutation (or subject line) at the left margin; **(c)** on the second line below the salutation (or subject line) indented 5 spaces.   2. ____1344a____

3. How many blank lines should be left between paragraphs: **(a)** 1; **(b)** 2; **(c)** none?   3. ____1344e____

4. When a three-line paragraph falls at the bottom of a page that is running long, you can carry one or two lines over to the top of the next page—**(a)** true; **(b)** false.   4. ____1344i____

5. Type the complimentary closing **(a)** on the second line below the message, starting at the left margin; **(b)** on the second line below the message, starting at the center; **(c)** on the third line blow the message, starting at the center.   5. ____1346a____

6. How many lines below the complimentary closing or the company signature should the writer's name ordinarily be typed: **(a)** 4; **(b)** 5; **(c)** 6?   6. ____1348a____

7. How should an 8½" × 11" sheet of stationery be folded for insertion in a No. 10 envelope: **(a)** in half; **(b)** in thirds; **(c)** in half, then in thirds?   7. ____1367a____

8. To hold the length of a memo to one page, you can reduce the top margin to **(a)** 1 inch; **(b)** 1.5 inches; **(c)** 1.75 inches.   8. ____1374b____

9. In a memo, a salutation should **(a)** always be used; **(b)** never be used; **(c)** be used whenever you want to keep the memo from seeming cold or impersonal.   9. ____1374l, note____

10. It is not necessary for e-mail messages to comply with the normal rules of written English—**(a)** true; **(b)** false.   10. ____1376a, d____

11. When you are sending an e-mail message to people who do not know each other, enter their names in **(a)** the *To* box; **(b)** the *Cc* box; **(c)** the *Bcc* box.   11. ____1379b____

Directions: Most of the items in the next exercise represent elements in a business letter. If the item is correctly styled, write *C* in the answer column. If not, rewrite the item to make it correct. Assume the use of a **modified-block style—standard format** (¶1302a), **standard punctuation** (¶1308a), and **single spacing** unless otherwise indicated. **References:** Section 13, plus ¶363, ¶455a, and ¶503.

12. Inside address and salutation: rewrite to avoid the use of an attention line and *Gentlemen.*   12. _____

```
Ace Programming Associates
221 Jefferson Street, NE
Albany, Oregon 97321-2717
Attention: Ms. Wanda Lee Belcher
Gentlemen:
```
1337a
1339a
1340
1341b

13. Subject. Long-range plans

14. We have two options to consider:

    1. Rent the VCR for one month
and see how well it works.

15. Cordially Yours:

16. *Ms. Joanna Wall*

    (Ms.) Joanna Wall

17. *Rae H. Zion*

    Mrs. Gerard U. Zion

18. Writer's identification:

    Dr. Henry Greco, Ph.D., Professor
       of Economics

19. fgc:ssh
    Encs. 3
    cc. Ms. Wing
    Certified

20. PS: All best regards to Pat.

21. Page 2
    Miss Selma L. Pomfret
    11/7/07

22. Address block typed on an envelope:

    Dwight G. Thorvald, Executive
       Vice President
    Winger Corp., Inc. *(official form not known)*
    651 East Neversink Rd.
    Suite 302
    Reading, Pa. 19606 3208

23. Heading typed on a memo:

    TO: Linda Lopez
    DEPARTMENT: Accounting
    SUBJECT: Invoice No. 24396

24. Salutation in a social-business letter:

    Dear Jennifer:

---

13. _____ 1343c   363

14. _____
_____
_____
_____ 1344f
_____ 1345c

15. _____ 1346b

16. _____
_____ 1352b

17. _____
_____ 1352e

18. _____ 1350a
_____ 1350b
_____ 1349b

19. _____
_____ 1355a–c
_____ 1358b
_____   503
_____ 1359a
_____ 1361a–f

20. _____ 1365b

21. _____
_____
_____ 1366

22. _____
_____ 1368a
_____ 1322a
_____ 1325a
_____ 1329b
_____ 1317b
_____ 1337
_____ 1368f
_____ 1368c
_____ 1341a
_____ 1368d

23. TO: _____
DEPARTMENT: _____
                       1393f
SUBJECT: _____ 455a

24. _____ 1372b

28

Looking Things Up

Directions: Choose the phrase that best completes the meaning of the sentence. Then in the answer column record the identifying letter for the phrase you selected. **References:** Sections 12–18 and Appendixes A, B, C, and D.

1. When preparing a résumé, you should always indicate your age, your marital status, your height and weight, and your hobbies—**(a)** true; **(b)** false.

   1. _____ 1708k

2. When breaking a paragraph at the bottom of a page in a report, what is the minimum number of lines you must leave at the bottom of one page and carry over to the top of the next: **(a)** one; **(b)** two; **(c)** three?

   2. _____ 1407d 1407e

3. When you discover that you have a large number of e-mail messages that require a response, answer them in the order in which they were received, starting with the earliest—**(a)** true; **(b)** false.

   3. _____ 1387

4. Which is the best way to indicate that an apostrophe should be inserted in typed copy: **(a)** womens; **(b)** women's; **(c)** women s? *(Insert apostrophe)*

   4. _____ 1206

5. If it is not possible to communicate a negative assessment to a person face to face, it is acceptable to do so in an e-mail message—**(a)** true; **(b)** false.

   5. _____ 1382i-j

6. Which is the preferred pronunciation for *liaison:* **(a)** lee-YAY-zahn; **(b)** LAY-uh-zahn; **(c)** LEE-uh-zahn?

   6. _____ App. B

7. What is the most formal salutation you can use when writing to a woman you do not know: **(a)** Madam:; **(b)** Dear Madam:; **(c)** To whom it may concern:?

   7. _____ 1801e

8. If the column heads in a table do not all take the same number of lines, align the column heads **(a)** at the top; **(b)** at the bottom.

   8. _____ 1621g

9. Type quoted material as a displayed, single-spaced extract when it will make at least **(a)** four typed lines; **(b)** six; **(c)** eight.

   9. _____ 1424d 265a

10. When starting the first page of a new chapter, a table of contents, or a bibliography in a manuscript or a report, leave a top margin of **(a)** 1 inch; **(b)** 1.5 inches; **(c)** 2 inches.

    10. _____ 1405a 1415b 1548a

11. When a column of figures represents percentages, type a percent sign (%) after **(a)** the first percentage only; **(b)** each percentage.

    11. _____ 1630a

12. Which of the following represents an elliptical sentence: **(a)** Why not? **(b)** Drive slow. **(c)** Who cares?

    12. _____ App. D

13. In an e-mail message, the abbreviation *BTW* stands for **(a)** before the Web; **(b)** big time waster; **(c)** by the way.

    13. _____ 1382m

14. When typing a report that is bound, leave a left margin of **(a)** 1 inch; **(b)** 1.5 inches; **(c)** 2 inches.

    14. _____ 1404b

Directions: In the spaces provided, construct endnotes or bibliographic entries—as directed—for a specific book, using the following information: the title is *Safe Strategies for Financial Freedom;* the author is Van K. Tharp; the book was published in New York in 2004 by McGraw-Hill; the page numbers to be cited are 88, 89, 90, and 91; the price is $24.95.

15. Construct a business-style endnote referring to the Tharp book, and assign it the number 4.

_____

_____

1513a
1526a
1529b
460d

16. Recast the endnote above to agree with the typical academic style.

_____

_____

1513b
1536b

17. Make a subsequent reference in business style to the Tharp book in endnote 7. Cite page 104.

_____

1531a

18. Recast the subsequent reference above, using a formal academic style.

_____

1531d

19. Construct an appropriate entry for the Tharp book in a business-style bibliography.

_____

_____

1551a

20. Recast the entry above, using an academic style.

_____

_____

1551c

Directions: For each group of names or abbreviations given below, give the two-letter Postal Service abbreviations. (Study the chart on page 388 or the inside back cover of *The Gregg Reference Manual* ahead of time, and complete this exercise from memory.)

21.

Calif.	_____	Ala.	_____	Del.	_____	Ind.	_____
Fla.	_____	Colo.	_____	Okla.	_____	Oreg.	_____
Mass.	_____	Ill.	_____	Idaho	_____	Wis.	_____
Ohio	_____	Nebr.	_____	Mich.	_____	Wyo.	_____
Utah	_____	Wash.	_____	Ark.	_____	Guam	_____

22.

D.C.	_____	S. Dak.	_____	N.J.	_____	N.C.	_____
N. Mex.	_____	N.H.	_____	S.C.	_____	W. Va.	_____
R.I.	_____	P.R.	_____	N. Dak.	_____	N.Y.	_____

23.

Conn.	_____	La.	_____	Maine	_____	Hawaii	_____
Iowa	_____	Ga.	_____	Ky.	_____	Kans.	_____
Va.	_____	Pa.	_____	Md.	_____	Vt.	_____

24.

Ariz.	_____	Nev.	_____	Minn.	_____	Alaska	_____
Tex.	_____	Tenn.	_____	Mont.	_____	Mo.	_____
Miss.	_____						

29

Editing Practice A

Directions: Edit the following letter (typed in modified-block style—standard format with standard punctuation). Correct any errors in style, grammar, usage, spelling, content, and format. Circle any changes you make within the lines or out in the margin; if you prefer, show all changes on a separate sheet, identified by line number. If time permits, retype the corrected letter on a plain sheet of paper, using 1.25-inch side margins. (Assume you are using a printed letterhead, and leave a 2-inch top margin.) Use today's date and address the letter to *Lloyd I. Poindexter, Chief Executive Officer, Beck & McCall Advertising Agency, 3017 East Wacker Drive, Chicago, Illinois 60601.* **References:** Sections 1–13.

```
Dear Mister Poindexter,                                              17
                                                                     18
A few days ago you asked me to reccommend a qualified candidate to become    19
Director of Client Services. I can readily suggest Douglas Dichter.          20
                                                                     21
Doug majored in marketing at Northwestern, and recieved an MBA from Stanford 22
in 1996. He worked for awhile as a management consultant in the Pittsburg    23
office of Lyon & Waite Associates, but he found few opportunitys to put his  24
creative talents to use. In 2000, he joined Belles and Vissels, a small      25
advertising agency in Cincinatti, as a copywriter. In that capacity he was   26
responsible for coming up with the brand name Scratch for a new line of      27
cake mixs. (Remember the slogan? "It's not store bought. I made it from      28
Scratch"!) Among his other creative achievements were the name Pit Stop      29
for an under-arm deodorant. Doug was also responsible for The Inside         30
Scoop (a profitable chain of stores selling ice cream and frozen yogurt      31
and The Emotional Outlet (a successful department store that has attracted   32
a large amount of impulsive shoppers). After 2 years he became an account    33
executive and brought in 1,000,000's of dollars in new business. As a re-   34
sult, the Agency's reputation and size has undergone extroardinary growth.   35
Doug's boss gives him the lions share of the credit.                        36
                                                                     37
Doug is now ready to move on to more bigger challenges. Because of his       38
in depth experience in keeping a wide range of clients happy, his proven     39
skill in generating new business and his demonstrated maturity of judge-    40
ment, I think Doug would be well-qualified for the job you have in mind.     41
                                                                     42
I should note that Doug is married to my oldest daughter, but that does      43
not effect my ability to be objective about my son in law's qualifications.  44
However if you would like another opinion, why don't you write to Doug's     45
boss, Ms. Rhoda Colt. She knows of his eagerness to move to a higher level   46
position and can give you her own assessment of his past performance and     47
his future potential. If I can be of any farther assistence, let me know.    48
                                                                     49
                    Sincerely Yours                                  50
                                                                     51
                                                                     52
                                                                     53
          Mr. Buford J. Bellows                                      54
```

Directions: On the reverse side of this sheet you will find a letter to **Mr. Anthony J. Leonardo** (typed in modified-block style—standard format with standard punctuation). Correct any errors in style, grammar, usage, spelling, content, and format. Make the corrections as you did in the letter above. If time permits, retype the corrected letter on a plain sheet of paper, using 1.25-inch side margins and positioning the date on the first line below a 2-inch top margin. **References:** Sections 1–13.

Name _____ Date _____ Class _____ 59

Telekinetics
UNLIMITED

3334 CHAPEL HILL BOULEVARD
DURHAM, NORTH CAROLINA 27707
PHONE 919-555-6226
FAX 919-555-6313
WEB WWW.TELEKINETICS.COM

Feb. 7th 2007   **13**
                                                  14
                                                  15
                                                  16
Anthony J. Leonardo   **17**
111 Horton Rd.   **18**
Durham, NC, 27712   **19**
                                                  20
Dear Mr. Lenardo: **21**
                                                  22
I'd like to respond to you telephone message of Febuary forth in which   **23**
you asked for help in selecting a facsimile machine for you're home   **24**
office. Enclosed is a brochure that announces a one months' sale on   **25**
all of the fax equipment that we have available for immediate delivery.   **26**
Let me highlight a few items in that brochure.   **27**
                                                  28
1 Our most popular fax machine — the Faxiomatic 2000 (Model FA4098—   **29**
has a 30 page automatic document feeder, and a transmission speed   **30**
of 4 seconds a page. Normally listed at $499, it is available   **31**
during the month of February for $179, a saving of $320.00!   **32**
                                                  33
2 An even more versatile machine is the Artifax 777, which has a three   **34**
second transmission speed and a 256-shade gray scale. Thanks to a   **35**
58-1/4 % discount, the price of this machine (Model A777-2F) has been   **36**
slashed from $475 to $198.   **37**
                                                  38
3 Other models provide extra features such as automatic redialing and   **39**
delayed transmission (to let you take advantage of lower phone rates).   **40**
Sale prices range from $249-299.   **41**
                                                  42
    Come into see these models by February 28 the last day you can enjoy **43**
these special prices. Anyone of our salespeople can help you select the   **44**
equipment that's right for your home office and does not excede your bud- **45**
budget. Of course if you prefer you can ask for Stephen Burgos our Sales **46**
Manager or for myself. We'll be glad to help you in anyway that we can.   **47**
                                                  48
                        Sincerely   **49**
                                                  50
                                                  51
                                                  52
                        Julia G. Hough   **53**
                        Vice President of Sales   **54**
                                                  55
ybj   **56**
Enclosure   **57**

30

Editing Practice B

Directions: Edit the following letter (typed in modified-block style—with indented paragraphs and standard punctuation). Correct any errors in style, grammar, usage, spelling, content, and format. Circle any changes you make within the lines or out in the margin; if you prefer, show all changes on a separate sheet, identified by line number. If time permits, retype the corrected letter on a plain sheet of paper, using 1.25-inch side margins and starting on the first line below a 2-inch top margin. Use *Sincerely* for the complimentary closing, and type an appropriate signature line for *Ms. Angela R. Terlizzi.* **References:** Sections 1–13.

```
                        328 Linden Street                        13
                        Winnetka IL 60093                        14
                        October 23 2007                          15
                                                                 16
                                                                 17
                                                                 18
President                                                        19
New Computer Technologys Inc.                                    20
5,120 N Northwest Highway                                        21
Chicago, ILL 60631                                               22
                                                                 23
Dear Sir:                                                        24
                                                                 25
Can you please help me. During your semi-annual sale last Summer, a     26
pleasant salesman named Nick Fry helped me select a computer, and       27
persuaded me to order a specially-priced high speed printer that was    28
not on display in your showroom. What sold me on his reccommendation    29
was Mr. Frys' claim that this printer could turn out 40 pages a min-    30
minute. The computer was delivered in a few days, but it took more      31
then five weeks for the printer to arrive. When I hooked it up, I made  32
the shocking discovery that this printer actually turns out only 10 pages  33
a minute.                                                        34
                                                                 35
    I immediately called Mr. Fry to tell him that the printer was not    36
acceptable, but he was reluctant to take it back because he said it had  37
been specially ordered for me. He offered to sell me a special attach-   38
ment that would increase the speed of the printer, but I refused to spend  39
any more money on it. He finely agreed to take the printer back but said  40
he would have to impose an $85.00 "restocking charge" against my refund  41
because I had removed the printer from the carton and used it. I pointed  42
out that 1) it was his misrepresentation that had cause the problem, I    43
had relied on his know how, and 3) the charge was totally unjustified.   44
I still don't have my moneyback, and I still don't have a useable printer.  45
Would you be able to follow-up with the appropriate people to get this    46
problem promptly resolved? I sincerly hope so.                   47
```

Directions: On the reverse side of this sheet you will find the second page of a letter to **Mr. Richard L. Booker Jr.** (typed in modified-block style—standard format with standard punctuation) and the No. 6¾ envelope that accompanies it. Correct any errors in style, grammar, usage, spelling, content, and format. Make the corrections as you did in the letter above. If time permits, retype the letter on a plain sheet of paper, using 1.25-inch side margins and starting the heading for the second page on the first line below a 1-inch top margin. Retype the envelope copy on a No. 6¾ envelope or on a sheet of paper trimmed or ruled off to the same dimensions. **References:** Sections 1–13.

Name _____ Date _____ Class _____ 61

derstanding of the different kinds of businesses that this organization has aquired or built from the ground up.

In short within the next 3 months we need to hire a Director of Corporate Planning and Development with at least ten year's experience in a large, industrial corporation. Because of our need to compete more effectively in global markets we would give preferrence to a candidate who: 1) has worked for a multi-national organization, 2) adjusts easily to a variety of corporate cultures, and 3) is proficient in one or more foreign languages (particularly Japanese, German and French.) The successful candidate will report directly to the CEO, but he must be a bright, energetic self starter who does not need others to set goals and prioritys. It's not going to be easy to find someone who meets all the qualifications in the enclosed job description Rich, but if anyone can locate the ideal person, your the one who can do it.

                        Sincerely,

                        P.J. McInerny
                        Executive Vice President

pac
By certified mail
Enclosure

P. J. Macinery

CHESHIRE INDUSTRIES INC.
1200 North Market Street
Wilmington, Delaware 19801

                                                    Personal

                Mr. Richard L. Booker, Jr.
                Kopf-Jaeger International
                Suite 450
                1150 Connecticut Avenue, N. W.
                Washington, D.C. 20036

31

Editing Practice C

Directions: Read the following letter (typed in **block style** with standard punctuation). Correct any errors in style, grammar, usage, spelling, content, and format. Circle any changes you make within the lines or out in the margins; if you prefer, show all changes on a separate sheet, identified by line number. If time permits, retype the corrected letter on a plain sheet of paper, using 1.25-inch side margins. Use *Jennifer A. Warren* for the writer's typed signature. (Assume you are using a computer-generated letterhead, and type today's date on the first line below a top margin of 2 inches.)
References: Sections 1–13.

```
Mr. Peter Q. Dorian                                                17
1 Eagle Sq.                                                        18
Concord, N.H. 03301                                               19
                                                                   20
Dear Pete:                                                         21
                                                                   22
George and I are now ready to go foreword with the vacation house we   23
discussed with you last Spring. You'll recall that our hideaway is to  24
be built on a 1¹/₂ acre plot atop Mt. Waumbeck. It's not an easy place 25
to get to, because the unpaved road that leads from the highway to our 26
property is a narrow twisting lane. We're planning to name our moun-   27
mountain retreat Great Lengths, so if any of our children and their    28
familys want to visit us there, they'll have to go to . . . I think you 29
get the point.                                                         30
                                                                   31
Can you design a log cabin for George and I. I don't know whether you  32
have worked with logs before but a recent Smithsonian article says that 33
the log cabin is making a real come-back. Largely as a result of the   34
back to the earth movement that started in the 1960's. Then the fuel   35
crisis in the 70's prompted the development of new types of sealants   36
and caulkings. This means that the log cabins being built today can    37
project the pioneer look of the past and meet the energy efficient     38
needs of the future at the same time.                                  39
                                                                   40
Once we get the plans from you we are thinking of building the cabin    41
ourselves. It doesn't sound to hard. In fact, one person refered to    42
in the Smithsonian article made this comment: "To build a log cabin,   43
all you need are a good chain saw and a good chiropractor."            44
                                                                   45
We weren't planning to cut the logs ourselves. There are kits you can  46
buy, but the logs we looked at seemed too uniform in appearance. We    47
have found a great sawmill in nearby Jefferson that has offerred to     48
cut the logs in accordance with your plans.                            49
                                                                   50
When can we get together with you to discuss the rough sketches we have 51
made? We'll be glad to drive into your office in Concord or if you pre- 52
fer to your studio in Hopkinton. We are free most Wensdays from 7:30-   53
9:00 p.m. in the evening. Just say the word and we'll be there.        54
                                                                   55
                    Sincerely,                                     56
```

Directions: On the reverse side of this sheet you will find a memo concerning an upcoming sales conference at **The Homestead in Hot Springs, Virginia.** Correct any errors in style, grammar, usage, spelling, and format. Make the corrections as you did in the letter above. If time permits, retype the corrected memo on a plain sheet of paper, using 1-inch side margins and starting on the first line below a 1-inch top margin. **References:** ¶¶1373–1374 (on memos), Section 16 (on tables), plus Sections 1–12.

Name _____ Date _____ Class _____   63

INTEROFFICE MEMORANDUM

To:	Tiffany N. Cartier	**From:**	Ben G. Opalewski
Department:	Conference Services	**Department:**	Southern Region
Subject:	Southern Sales Conference	**Date:**	June 14, 2007

Dear Tifany:

This is a follow up to my memo of June 6th. The site for the Southern Regions' sales conference has now seen selected: a five star hotel in Hot Springs Virginia called The Homestead. The conference will start at 7:00 P.M. on Tuesday, August 7 with a formal dinner on the terrace (weather permiting.) The meeting will end at 12 noon on Saturday, the 11th, we'll skip the closing luncheon this year so that everyone can get an earlier start for home. Sounds alright so far, doesn't it.

Here comes the fun part. In addition, to the handouts that should be run off, (we discussed these last week) about sixty-five slides need to be made up. Could you get Jenny Ziff in graphic arts to do these for us. She did a first rate job on slides for our mid Febuary meeting.

At the August meeting we'll have to supply our own AV equipment I'm sorry to say. The Conference Director at The Homestead has told me that most all their equipment are committed to two other groups meeting during the same week. Therefore I'd appreciate if you could have the following items deliverred to the hotel, and if you could be on hand to help the speakers at the conference.

Schedule	AV Equipment	Speaker
Wednesday, Session 1	DVD player and VCR; 3 color monitors (largest size available	Oberholtzer
Thursday, Session 5	Computer projector plus screen*	Potterfield
Friday, Session 9	Wireless microphone plus speakers; easel with pad	Velasquez

---

*Potterfeld may also want a digital camcorder to record some role playing situations, he'll let us know by July 20.

The other speakers all say they need no equipment, so be prepared for last-minute requests. Thanks Tiffany for your help and your patients.

BGO

lcd

Editing Practice D

Directions: Edit the following letter to **Dr. Prescott T. Daley** (typed in modified-block style—standard format with standard punctuation). Correct any errors in style, grammar, usage, spelling, content, and format. Circle any changes you make within the lines or out in the margin; if you prefer, show all changes on a separate sheet, identified by line number. If time permits, retype the corrected letter on a plain sheet of paper, using 1.25-inch side margins. (Assume you are using a printed letterhead, and leave a 2-inch top margin.) Use the current date, use *Sincerely* as the complimentary closing, and prepare an appropriate signature block for *Ms. Joyce L. Givens, director of alumni programs.* Supply reference initials and any other notations that may be appropriate. **References:** Section 1–13.

```
Dr. Prescott T. Daley, M.D.                                        17
2,901 N. Central Ave.                                              18
Phoenix, AR, 85012                                                19
                                                                  20
Dear Dr. Daly:                                                    21
                                                                  22
We are please to announce a special alumni program that offers unusual   23
travel and study opportunities. Between June 3-13 Cary O. Neilson, a     24
Professor of English who specializes in English Literature of the 18th   25
century will lead a tour through the Western counties of England. An     26
engaging and entertaining lecturer, Professor Neilson will help you see  27
the land and its people through the eyes of Jane Austen, William Shake-  28
speare and other great English writers.                                  29
                                                                  30
The trip begins on Wednesday, June 3 with a departure from the U.S. on   31
a regularly-scheduled flight to Heathrow airport. You will then travel   32
by motor coach to Bath, where you will have accomodations at the elegant 33
Francis Hotel for the first 4 nights. The mineral springs at Bath have   34
made this a fashionable gathering place since roman times. From Bath     35
you will embark on a full day excursion to the cathedral town of Salis-  36
bury. You will continue onto Stonehenge, the 4000 year old circle of     37
massive stones that draw all visitors into the continuing debate about   38
the original purpose of this monument. Your itinery will next take you   39
to Stratford, the site of William Shakespeares' home. On the morning of  40
June 13 you will be taken back to Heathrow for a return flight to the    41
United States. Throughout your trip Professor Neilson will offer an      42
educational program of lectures and reading materials that make signifi- 43
cant references to all the places you will visit.                        44
                                                                  45
The enclosed brochure provides a detailed description of the itinerary,  46
the rate schedules, and the activities planed by Professor Neilson.      47
Because I made the trip last year I think I can answer any questions     48
you may have about the trip. May we reserve a place for you?             49
```

Directions: On the reverse side of this sheet you will find a page taken from a business report on information processing (with business-style footnotes). Correct any errors in style, grammar, usage, spelling, content, and format (including spacing). Make the corrections as you did in the letter above. If time permits, retype the corrected page on a plain sheet of paper, using 1.25-inch side margins and starting on the first line below a 1-inch top margin. **References:** Sections 14–15 plus Sections 1–12.

8

7
8
9
10
11
12
13
14
15
16
17
18
19
20
21
22
23
24
25
26
27
28
29
30
31
32
33
34
35
36
37
38
39
40
41
42
43
44
45
46
47
48
49
50
51
52
53
54
55
56
57
58
59
60

portunities will always be available in the feild of information processing for those who have good skills and can adapt to continual changes in the workplace. According to one authority:

> "Most people will change careers two to four times within their working lifetimes—and that statistic does not include job changes. The average working person . . . . will make five, six, or even more job changes in addition to career changes.[4]

Moreover, within the next ten to 15 years, between 20-50% of the available jobs will have titles and descriptions that do not now exist. [5] In other words not only will you be changing jobs in the course of your career, but the jobs themselves maybe changing as well. For that reason it is critical to develop skills that are transferrable from one job to another, and are not likely to be come obsolete.

CAREERS IN INFORMATION PROCCESSING

Within an organization there are typically three levels of jobs: opera- tors, assistants, and managers. In addition, there is a number of re- lated opportunitys outside the organization.[7]

Operators

Operator's jobs are usually classified according to the level of skill and experience required.

Information Processing Trainee. This is an entry level job that requires good keyboarding and formating skills but no experience. Un-

---

4. Sharon Lund O'Neil, *Office Information Systems: Concepts And Applications*, *3d ed.*, Glencoe, Westerville, Ohio, 1999, p. 292.

5. O'Neil, p. 300-1.
6. See appendix A for a full list of job titles and descriptions.

33 Final Survey

Directions: Correct the punctuation and capitalization in each sentence below. If the punctuation is incorrect, draw a line through it: *an old winter coat.* If new punctuation is to be inserted, circle it: *I too hope so.* To change a small letter to a capital letter, draw three lines under it: *Christmas.* To change a capital letter to a small letter, draw a line through it: *Enough.* If a sentence is correct as given, write *C* in the answer column. **References:** Sections 1–3.

1. Bob Lois and I want to find small aggressive companies we can invest in — 1. _____
2. May I please have two hours of your time on Monday May 6 to get some advice — 2. _____
3. Thanks for sending me a copy of your letter of March 4 in which you take the directors to task for approving excessive pay for top executives what a mess — 3. _____
4. The President of Gage seminars has asked how many managers you plan to send — 4. _____
5. Did you really exceed your sales goal by 40 percent unbelievable — 5. _____
6. It's odd, isn't it, how some people will buy a pre-owned vehicle but not a used car — 6. _____
7. Did the supplier who called on us last friday, send the additional data I asked for — 7. _____
8. In my judgment his son Ted lacks the managerial skills needed to run the Division — 8. _____
9. If your assistant is not that busy could she please help us with our backlog — 9. _____
10. We could rendezvous in Amherst New York or if you prefer in London Ontario — 10. _____
11. It is urgent therefore that we make a counteroffer to their President Fay Perry — 11. _____
12. Please supply the following data Purpose of loan amount needed duration of loan — 12. _____
13. Liza Lotte Ph.D. is writing the Company's history, and will be done this Fall — 13. _____
14. The transaction meets State laws but will it satisfy Federal regulations — 14. _____
15. Before I came back east last Winter I worked for a large, mining company in Utah. — 15. _____
16. You don't think our profit shortfall will go as high as $1000000 do you — 16. _____
17. We must therefore ask for a deposit even though your credit rating is good — 17. _____
18. We can't find the will but we do have the codicil dated december 6 2004. — 18. _____
19. Paul do you think Dan Peters the President of NDG would be a good CEO for us — 19. _____
20. In 2004 Farley Mudge Jr. made a substantial investment in Ariel Inc. — 20. _____
21. To enter a subscription call 1-800-555-0600 to renew one call 1-800-555-0602 — 21. _____
22. Whenever I tell Charlie that I need his help he says can it wait — 22. _____
23. (See section 2 a land to be fought for in exodus from the desert — 23. _____
24. The demonstration sites are: Ames Iowa Bath Maine and Logan Utah — 24. _____
25. The layouts look great to me however ask the marketing department to okay them — 25. _____
26. Could someone from the Center For Auto Safety pick me up at Reagan airport — 26. _____
27. He teaches french history, and is an authority on the eighteenth century for example he did a book on the Seventeen-Nineties and the french revolution — 27. _____
28. After I graduated I left Knoxville but I'm still fond of Eastern Tennessee — 28. _____
29. The CEO along with his staff will host a party on the fourth of July — 29. _____
30. An "ad hoc" committee was set up in July 2005 or was it August — 30. _____

Name _____ Date _____ Class _____ 67

Directions: The following items deal with problems in number style, abbreviations, plural and possessive forms, spelling, compound words, and word division. (*Note:* The symbol / is used in items 96–100 to show word division at the end of a line.) If an item is correct as given, write *C* in the answer column. If an item is incorrect, circle the error and show the correct form in the answer column. **References:** Sections 4–9.

31. got 12 PCs (6 are laptops)	_____	66. defered this payment	_____
32. after July 31st	_____	67. a cancelled check	_____
33. had to pay over $200.00	_____	68. an acknowledgment	_____
34. with a unit cost of $.86	_____	69. quite an acheivement	_____
35. for now. 20 years ago . . .	_____	70. very persistant	_____
36. before the 20th century	_____	71. may now procede	_____
37. is more than 1/2 done	_____	72. submit your resume	_____
38. in two-liter containers	_____	73. our principle goal	_____
39. reduced benefits before 65	_____	74. to forego an increase	_____
40. a thirty-day grace period	_____	75. can't except his excuse	_____
41. almost fifty years ago	_____	76. to wave one's rights	_____
42. opens at nine A.M.	_____	77. was basicly correct	_____
43. consulted R.M. Siu	_____	78. try to accomodate	_____
44. Doctor Baldwin's opinion	_____	79. it looks familar	_____
45. an S.E.C. ruling	_____	80. highly reccommended	_____
46. US Department of Energy	_____	81. need your good will	_____
47. a trip to Washington, D.C.	_____	82. let's check-up on it	_____
48. 6 lbs. @ $8.25	_____	83. read the print-outs	_____
49. only a 100-km. drive	_____	84. good at problem solving	_____
50. entertain a VIP.	_____	85. wants it triple spaced	_____
51. unexpected tendencys	_____	86. a high pressure job	_____
52. when the attornies meet	_____	87. a three-year's lease	_____
53. invite husbands and wifes	_____	88. my income-tax return	_____
54. console the runner-ups	_____	89. our toll free number	_____
55. a strange phenomena	_____	90. found it nerve racking	_____
56. sold by the Connollys	_____	91. was too fast paced	_____
57. back in the 1990's	_____	92. a newly decorated office	_____
58. the witness's account	_____	93. bring me up-to-date	_____
59. took Jo Barne's place	_____	94. let's re-elect her	_____
60. both agencies' accounts	_____	95. much too self confident	_____
61. a sale on womens' coats	_____	96. we stop-/ ped going	_____
62. it's Harry's, not their's	_____	97. on sep-/ arate checks	_____
63. Ed and Fran's signatures	_____	98. an exped-/ ient action	_____
64. need two dollars worth	_____	99. was transferr-/ ing	_____
65. ask about me getting a job	_____	100. sell-/ ing at a loss	_____

Directions: Underline all errors and write the correct forms in the answer column. If a sentence is correct as given, write *C* in the answer column. **References:** Sections 10–11.

101. Every sales rep and field manager have to be notified at once.

101. _____

102. Only one of the fax machines are in service right now.

102. _____

103. Was any of the incoming phone calls from Mrs. Malifitano?

103. _____

104. Our criteria for establishing a customer's creditworthiness has changed.

104. _____

105. The number of calls about equipment breakdowns is unacceptable.

105. _____

106. Bob is one of those people who assumes you always have time to talk.

106. _____

107. None of the position papers deal with the impact on employee morale.

107. _____

108. I wish I was able to devote time to the company's tutoring program.

108. _____

109. When will the company update their policy on environmental issues?

109. _____

110. Between you and I, the board isn't very happy with the new CEO.

110. _____

111. Moira seems to think she's better qualified to do my job than me.

111. _____

112. Mike and myself expect our funding proposal to be approved.

112. _____

113. Whom do you think is the leading authority on artificial intelligence?

113. _____

114. We had a real nice time at the Benzingers' reception.

114. _____

115. I feel very bad about losing the lease on my store.

115. _____

116. We never participated in no meetings with the Finley brothers.

116. _____

117. It's too early to tell whether the rail strike will effect us.

117. _____

118. We've had an excessive amount of complaints on those bearings.

118. _____

119. Business was slow for awhile, but orders are starting to pick up.

119. _____

120. In recent weeks I've made less mistakes.

120. _____

Directions: Rewrite the following sentences to correct all errors. **References:** Primarily Sections 10–11.

121. Every salesman should continuously monitor his travel expenses. _____

_____

122. We not only reviewed this years' sales patterns but also last year. _____

_____

123. Neither the employees nor the supervisor has met his production quota. _____

_____

124. To open an account, this card should be filled out. And returned to us. _____

_____

125. The will's provisions have been challenged by everyone of us relatives. _____

_____

Directions: On the reverse side of this sheet you will find a letter to **Mr. Ferris G. Hartmann** (typed in modified-block style—standard format with standard punctuation). Correct all errors in style, grammar, and format; also look for errors in typing and content. Circle all changes you make within the lines or out in the margins; if you prefer, show all changes on a separate sheet, identified by line number. If time permits, retype the corrected letter on a plain sheet of paper, using 1.25-inch side margins and positioning the date on the first line below a 2-inch top margin. **References:** Sections 13 plus Sections 1–12. See also pages 358–359 or the inside back cover of *The Gregg Reference Manual* for a chart showing how to indicate corrections on typed material.

Name _____ Date _____ Class _____ 69

Highlawn Hills

P.O. Box 455 Sparta, NJ 07871 Phone: 973.555-5675 Fax: 973.555-5890 Web: www.hhills.com

Feb. 16 2007   **13**
                                                               14
                                                               15
                                                               16
Ferris G. Hartmann   **17**
1,516 S.W. 10th St.   **18**
Topeka, KS 66604   **19**
                                                               20
Dear Mr. Hartman: **21**
                                                               22
    Thank you for your letter of February sixth in which you expressed **23**
some interest in acquiring a one family home in Highlawn Hills. Since **24**
you and your wife will not be visiting the Sparta area until later in **25**
the Spring let me try to answer some of your questions now.   **26**
                                                               27
1 The community consists entirely of custom-crafted 2, 3, and 4-bedroom **28**
houses, artfully-blended into an 800-acre hilltop setting and priced from **29**
$335,000-$595,000. In short every house enjoys a million-dollar view **30**
without the million-dollar price tag.   **31**
                                                               32
2 Highlawn Hills has been created by the Saroyan Brothers Development **33**
Company, master builders of award-winning communities with more than **34**
thirty years experience. Every house contains such amenities as a wood **35**
burning fireplace, a sundeck, sun-filled skylights and 2-1/2 bathrooms **36**
(including a jacuzzi in the master bathroom.   **37**
                                                               38
3 Every family in Highlawn Hills can enjoy the following on-site faci- **39**
lities; an 18-hole golf course, tennis courts, an Olympic-sized swiming **40**
pool, jogging trails, and a clubhouse with a fitness center. At a near- **41**
by shopping center are a gourmet supermarket, two department stores, and **42**
a number of elegant boutiques. Moreover, your children will have excess **43**
to a school district that is rated one of the best in the State. **44**
                                                               45
I'm enclosing a prospectus, that describes all the propertys now being **46**
offerred for sale. Also enclosed is a booklet about Sparta, and a bro- **47**
chure describing the lovely unspoiled setting of Highlawn Hills. When **48**
you do come to Sparta, why don't you give me a call. Either Farley Fox, **49**
our Sales Manager or I would be please to help you in anyway we can. **50**
                                                               51
                        Cordialy Yours   **52**
                                                               53
                                                               54
                                                               55
                        Paula B. Sharpe   **56**
                        Associate sales manager   **57**
                                                               58
Enclosures 2   **59**
was   **60**

70